John Maher
of
Delancey Street

John Maher
of
Delancey Street

A GUIDE TO PEACEFUL
REVOLUTION IN AMERICA

by GROVER SALES

W · W · NORTON & COMPANY · INC ·
NEW YORK

❲ The text type in this book is Linotype Electra with Electra oblique.
Composition, printing, and binding are by the Vail-Ballou Press, Inc.

First Edition

Library of Congress Cataloging in Publication Data
Sales, Grover.
    John Maher of Delancey Street.
    1. Maher, John, 1940–   2. Delancey Street
Foundation.   3. Halfway houses—San Francisco.
I. Title.
HV9306.S42D47   362.2'93'0924 [B]   75-35880

ISBN 0 393 07499 4

1 2 3 4 5 6 7 8 9 0

To Charles E. Dederich, who worked
the miracle
and Georgia MacLeod Sales, whose love and
guidance made the book possible.

Contents

Photographs appear following page 80.

"The Wobblies were the prophets and forerunners of a new religion. Every religion starts at the bottom level, with the whores, publicans and sinners. Logically it has to start there, with the dissatisfied. You can't get the satisfied to accept new ideas. . . . The new religion will come here in America, because it is here in America, the home of the most hated race where the hope of the world will lie. The greatest religions always come up out of the most hated races."

—Jack Malloy in *From Here to Eternity*

"Even as a kid, when my brother John stood in front of you, you knew immediately that here was somebody you had to *deal* with, you couldn't ignore."

—Billy Maher

"The worse they were on the street, the better they are when we clean 'em up."

—Chuck Dederich, founder of Synanon

"All leaders, good or bad, who successfully promoted social movements, started with nothing: Martin Luther King, Jesus, Gandhi, Mao, Hitler, and Buddha—a millionaire prince who had to give it all away before he could get anything going. The Mormon empire is the classic case of a fanatical, oppressed, and impoverished people who could build an economic power *independent* of the government.

"If a group of addicts and convicts can organize, with no violence, along multi-racial lines, and produce an economically cooperative situation—health care, employment, education—without the endless 'help' of professional social workers and the government—this means that the myth of the impotence of the people has forever been put to rest."

—John Maher, founder of Delancey Street

Introduction

Nothing in John Maher's origins as a New York slum junkie points to his spectacular rise as founder of the Delancey Street Foundation, a community of former addicts and convicts that built a working model in San Francisco for a unique form of urban revolution.

Now thirty-five, Maher was first arrested at the age of eight for playing hookey. At ten he started to carry numbers slips and drugs. At twelve he was sent to reform school for burglary. For the next nine years he was in and out of "kiddie joints" and jails for narcotics possession and sale, armed robbery, breaking and entering, larceny, selling false draft cards, pickpocketing, and pimping.

At twenty-two he decided to kick his habit "because all the big-time gangsters I was trying to impress didn't trust junkies," and he spent his next eight years cleaning up in Synanon, California's radical new life-style center for ex-addicts. There he quickly rose to a directorship and built a following among Synanon's squares (nonaddicts), many of them rich and influential, who had been attracted to Charles E. "Chuck" Dederich's compelling social experiment.

Breaking with Synanon because he felt it had lost touch with its early revolutionary goals as well as its involvement with society, Maher started the Delancey Street Foundation in 1970 with $1,000 borrowed from loan sharks, the only group that would lend money to an ex-convict.

In less than four years he parlayed Delancey Street into a million dollar foundation and a front-page *cause célèbre*.

In the heart of San Francisco's richest and most protectively zoned residential area, he built an interracial community of three hundred former addicts living drug-free, nonviolent, law-abiding, and productively employed lives.

He put his people to work by organizing a chain of businesses that grossed $1.5 million in 1974: a roofing company, an auto repair shop, a construction and plumbing business, a moving company, an advertising specialties sales force, a florist shop and terrarium business, and a swank restaurant and bar in the city's most fashionable shopping area.

To house and employ Delancey's residents, Maher purchased three choice pieces of real estate worth $1.5 million and leased six buildings valued at $2.1 million. Most of these properties are in ultrarespectable neighborhoods.

Delancey Street became the first ex-convict group to be approved by a federal agency as a credit union—assets $30,000. The Foundation is now accredited as a high school and runs a vocational college to train real-estate brokers, computer technicians, and secretaries.

Maher is in demand throughout America and Europe as an authority on crime prevention, addiction, and prison reform. He has become a regular guest on national TV talk shows. Paramount Pictures filmed a TV special on Delancey Street. Social planners from France, England, Louisiana, Arkansas, and New York visit Delancey Street with an eye toword starting replicas in their own communities. They are struck by the obvious differences between Maher's group and other halfway houses. Pushing beyond the limited goals of the drug-cure center, Delancey Street aims to become a prime political force in San Francisco with the clout to elect sympathetic public officials and change laws. Maher has cemented ties with top labor unions; women's lib, gay lib, and senior citizens groups, the Prisoners' Union, the Farm Workers Union, the black community, and "the sane people working within our two major political parties" in San Francisco's City Hall, Sacramento, and the United States Congress.

Maher built this self-fueling economic power base—complete with food, clothing, housing, medical-dental care, education, entertainment, and job training—*independently* of federal aid, welfare, professional social workers, and large foundation funds.

Maher cajoles a steady flow of cash, goods, and services from a dedicated alliance of hard-hats, rich Jews, professors, bartenders, attorneys, union officials, artists, civic leaders, housewives, real-estate developers, disc jockies, ad executives, ministers, and socialites. His most vocal supporters and frequent guests include Dr. Karl Menninger, Herbert Gold, jazzmen Cal Tjader and Mongo Santamaria, San Francisco's reform sheriff Richard Hongisto, Congressman Philip Burton, Cesar Chavez, and California Assemblyman Willie Brown (who stands a chance of being elected San Francisco's first black mayor).

What sort of man, still in his early thirties, could build such an empire by marshaling the support of the most diverse elements in a fragmented society?

   * * * *

The author is indebted to Lewis Yablonsky's *Synanon: The Tunnel Back*, and Guy Endore's *Synanon* for material on the early days of Synanon.

John Maher

of

Delancey Street

CHAPTER ONE

The Neighborhood

"God is not to be fucked with."

John Maher is reluctant to talk about his past,
not because he's ashamed of it, but because it bores him.*

JOHN MAHER: My past? Why would anybody want to
hear about that? It's hackneyed to death, typical of a hundred thousand New York gutter rats. Only reason I'm
different is I'm lucky, I had the opportunity to get out. *Very
few do.*

*Eldest of four sons and a daughter of an Irish immigrant
working-class family, John came of age on the streets of the
Bronx. His father was an electrician for Con Edison and his
mother worked as a telephone operator. Of the four Maher
boys, only quiet, withdrawn Patrick never got into trouble.
Thomas is an addict currently in an Eastern jail for assault.
Kid brother Billy got hooked at fifteen, was in and out of
jail until he came to California, "cleaned up my act," managed Delancey Street's businesses, headed its Credit Union,
and now goes to law school.*

BILLY MAHER: Father liked to beat us and Mother liked
to play martyr. There was a complete divorce within the con-
text of living under the same roof. Father had his own shelf
in the icebox, his own bed in his own room. They were

* Pronounced MA'-her.

Catholic, but not terribly devout. Father didn't like children; he wanted Mother to sit in a gin mill with him, like all good Irish working proletariats do, but Mother had delusions of gentility and wanted to go to museums and plays. She owned a lot of the books, like Dickens and Thackeray, that John and I grew up reading. The only reason Father never left us was he felt it wasn't the right thing to do.

The first time I remember brother John, I was fourteen and he was twenty; he was always in reform school or jail when I was growing up. He'd come home from jail and usually bring another hype [addict] with him. Father was always threatening to throw him out of the house, but Mother would say, "He's our son—let him stay," but after a month or two, John would be gone.

Once John helped me out in a street fight. I was getting my ass kicked in by a gang of Puerto Ricans. John only weighed about ninety pounds, but he scared the living shit out of them. Even when he was very young, John was obviously someone that had to be *dealt* with, you couldn't ignore. That has never changed. In a lot of ways, he's the same now as he was ten years ago. Instead of ripping people off, he builds things, but the personality is the same.

John views his past and his family with the cool detachment of an anthropologist observing the rites of some remote aboriginal tribe. His childhood memories filter through a heavy overlay of what he has become.

JOHN MAHER: My brother Billy sees our family through the veneer of modern education. To one raised on *Portnoy,* Sociology 1-A, and the *New York Review of Books,* this is the way one phrases things to appear intelligent and liberated. The problem with our family was its shaky transition from the old immigrant values to the new American values —by mixing them both, Jack, my father, failed at both. He punched us around a little, beat us by standards that would horrify today's permissive parents, but certainly not Sicilian farmers or an old Jew from Warsaw. People like the Molly Maguires and the Wobblies lived by their hands and cracked their kids in the head. That was life—I thought *every*body's father did that! Neither of my parents spent a lot of time with me, five kids and had to work for a living, where's the time?

As for my father being "divorced," what my brother Billy doesn't realize is, that's the custom of the people. My father's misfortune is that his younger children have been educated in America, and rather than understand *his* society, they have chosen, as they grow up, to do what so many Americans have done—whine and pule about what a hard time they had.

In the twenties and before in New York, the ghettos for ethnic whites were similar to the ghettos for ethnic blacks; when I grew up, the bulk of my neighborhood was Irish— postmen, cops, dockworkers. To go to the Jewish or Italian section was to be in a foreign land, so I grew up with all the standard prejudices against Jews and blacks.

From the age of five, John's real family was the Neighborhood, and he learned early that hanging out with older guys was the quickest way to get status. This was hard for someone frail and puny, no good at fighting or stickball, but the Maher clan's gift of gab made John the center of any crowd.

ED TURNBULL (childhood friend of John Maher, a graduate of Delancey Street): John was an incredibly charming boy. Even as a kid there was never a dull moment around him. We lived around industrial parks that were interesting to explore, and John would describe them in ways to make them seem even more exciting, places of great mystery and imagination. There was this big coalyard, and he'd tell you about all kinds of mystical things he'd seen there at night, and if you gave him a dime, he'd take you there. He was shaking down younger kids who were afraid of him; I always gave him change when he asked me, because I liked him.

At ten, we'd tell these very bad dirty jokes, but John's were always the best and the funniest, and he told them better. Most of these kids grew up to be construction workers and sand hogs; they never had much respect for anyone smart, but John they didn't kid. They thought of him as a wise-ass, but fun to be around, someone to respect. He was a logical schemer; there was this neighborhood bully named Murphy, a really big guy who hung around the schoolyard and had a habit of violence. John organized the other kids and faced Murphy with a united front. John told him, "Murphy, from now on, if you go after *any one* of us, we'll *all* jump you and kick the shit out of you." That was the end of Murphy.

When John got in trouble on the street, his father would lock him in his room for weeks at a time. John spent the time reading.

JOHN MAHER: Everyone in the family read; my father was addicted to detective novels, mother liked poetry, the whole family was smart. At seven I was thrilled with the adventures of Richard Halliburton, and later read James T. Farrell's *Studs Lonigan,* one of the first books where I could identify with the characters.

When I wasn't locked up in my room, I hung around the Public Library, where I found a copy of *Crime and Punishment*—that started me off at nine or ten on the Russians—Dostoevsky, Tolstoy, Pushkin, Turgenev, Gogol. I was knocked out by this kind of Russian romanticism and mysticism because it was closely related to the "Celtic twilight" attitude that was part of my family culture. Then I went through the classic Irish writers, Yeats, Singe, Swift, Shaw, and Joyce. I'd get involved in a genre and run through them almost by nationality; German authors from Goethe to Hitler; Rilke, Heine, Lessing, Mann. I read all of Dickens; he was fun, not a profound man, but a classic of a genre, like Groucho Marx. My grandmother bought the complete *Encyclopaedia Britannica* and the *Syntopicon* from some sweet-talking, door-to-door book hustler, and I read them, lots of history and geography, and became a quiz-kid type: "What would you like to know about Latvia, or the Ottoman Empire?"

In parochial school I was a defiant little bastard who delighted in tripping up the teachers, because by the seventh grade I was obviously better read than them. They didn't like that.

ED TURNBULL: John and I were together in St. Jerome's Grammar School from the ages of ten to fourteen; he was very knowledgeable about things not available in Catholic school history texts, and he read more advanced stuff, on the college level. When they told us that Betsy Ross made the first American flag, John would wise-off, "That's the wrong information." But instead of smacking him alongside the head like they'd do with anyone else, the Christian Brothers would smile and look at John with grudging admiration, because no matter how much of a wise guy he was, he could carry it off. He'd read behind-the-scenes books about the American Revolution and then get us out in the yard and run us the real information. John never did well on tests. He had a lot of information, but it was not the kind they wanted him to shovel back at them. He didn't read the schoolbooks and stood about eighth in the class; the kids who placed first and second were always dull boobs.

JOHN MAHER: These Catholic teachers were immature personalities who liked to be around children—possible homosexual panic. Even at the age of nine, I was aware they could not cut the mustard up at Maloney's Saloon. The Christian Brothers didn't have the religious convictions or the intelligence to become Jesuits, and they were too frightened by eternal damnation to go out and ball. The ones I saw, if they're *not* celebate, there's something wrong with American womanhood. They were the last effete remnants of a once-powerful theosophical-philosophical idea, but I

will say the Christian Brothers were much better "information givers" than the public schools, especially in that
crummy neighborhood. They taught you better how to read
and write, although their history was childish, like North
America was really civilized by Serra and Father Marquette.

Later I got into trouble in state training schools because
they tried to ply me with silly children's books—*The Story
of Pontius Pilate, In Illustrated Color*—so I got some good
old guy who worked there to bring me books. They usually
turned out to be mysteries, and I learned very early that
with mysteries, especially English drawing room and Sax
Rohmer stuff, the meter of the language would permit me as
a mimic to develop as a con merchant, which is what I've always been. In Sherlock Holmes, the English is always perfect. I can mimic, unconsciously, like a stage performer, any
ethnic or social type. Because I was a skinny child, and a bit
horrified at the barbarism around me, my style became whatever *you* were. I was the youngster in the room you could
identify with. I picked up the Yiddish underworld talk because I was trained by old Jewish pickpockets downtown,
learned all about Jewish dietary habits, so in the presence of
Jews I could do my Lower East Side number; among Irish,
Italians, and even blacks, it was the same. This was later
extended to social classes of the upper echelons—opinion
makers, financiers, society people, politicians, which has
stood me in good stead today.

A lot of my reading locked up at home, or in jail, had
to do with intellectual pretention, and creating an image
of myself as being smarter than other people in a world that
seemed impossible for me to control, much more of a
neurotic response than a true quest for learning. It terrified
adults and gave me *entré* into their world as a "cute freak,"
like a kid who can juggle good. I was a sociopathic child
who found in reading a tool, like boxing.

By the time of his first arrest for playing hooky, John used his learning and wit to impress an older group of role models —professional teen-age criminals, "real stand-up guys" steeped in the romance and close-to-the-vest traditions of the old-time thief. His early life was a round of breaking into apartments, boosting a coat out of Macy's, getting bombed on cheap gin, running away from home. At twelve he persuaded Ed Turnbull to join him.

ED TURNBULL: John led me through a playground and we climbed a fence on the elevated railway. He slid underneath the tracks into a cubbyhole he'd fixed up with rugs, sheets, and blankets he stole out of hallways and off clotheslines. It was freezing. We pulled this rug over us and went to sleep. About 6:00 A.M. I woke up; there was this tremendous roar, the first train of the morning. John went to the grocery and stole some fruit and milk—in those days they dropped the stuff right in front of the closed store, which they'd never dream of doing today. When John got tired of the cubbyhole, he'd sleep in cheap, vacant rooming houses.

JOHN MAHER: At twelve I graduated from running numbers slips to delivering dope; nobody'd suspect a skinny kid that young and angelic. The dealer would give me $1 and some small packets and say, "Deliver this to 144th Street." One day I copped one of the bags I was told to deliver, ran into a couple of older junkies, and said, "Look, show me how you do that," so they skin-popped me and got themselves some free junk. It made me violently ill the first time, and looking back I can see it got me a tremendous amount of attention. Once I was done throwing up, it was great to sit there and feel good. But even at that age I had already been drinking a year or two.

ED TURNBULL: John must have been working in the dope business, because he was always well dressed. While the other kids were wearing Levis in 1955, he was in very expensive three-button Ivy-League suits, well groomed as always, silk ties at age fifteen, very tasteful pinstripe Oxford suits. But then he'd cap it off with something weird and attention getting, like those skinny-brim hats that Puerto Ricans wore. He was pretty well hooked by fifteen on dope, which was unpopular in our neighborhood, the South Bronx, all Irish, where most of the kids was interested in growing up and drinking alcohol like their fathers. The big thing was to get a phony draft card so's you could get into a bar.

JOHN MAHER: I had a friend with a photographer's studio who reproduced these sought-after draft cards, or a birth certificate so's you could get a job. These guys in the photo lab would supply me with these phonies, which I'd hustle on the street to sixteen-year-old kids who want to drink in a bar, or to somebody fifteen who needs to be seventeen to get his working papers. Or they'd print up phony tickets to all the big Broadway shows and sporting events, and then I'd catch a "fish," a tourist, in the Roosevelt Hotel lobby. "I got these two tickets to this show and my Dad can't take me." The fish would always try to beat me down, "Ten buck ticket? I'll give you five," when he knew they were scalping for fifty bucks.

We made hooks out of coat hangers, put them up our sleeves and used them to open cars. Had a couple of dentist bits for picking locks, easy in those days because they had them long skeleton keys; you have to be a pro to pick a lock now. Had a couple of $20 bills on me at all times, to go into stores to shortchange people. Or sometimes a fool tourist was looking for a whore, so I'd sell him a nonexistent girl.

I was arrested for procuring at sixteen; they were having a crime wave on the West Side, Columbus Avenue, and cops were placing guys in Spanish bars acting drunk, for entrapment. I was selling nickle-and-dime junk, nothing big, and all these whores on the block would come score off me. Police thought I was pimping these broads, though this wasn't true at that time. I was living with a hooker much older than me. We were walking home one night, a cop comes over and asks, "Can I have this girl?" Didn't even wait for an answer, the cops grabbed me, threw me in the car, and let the girl go. Gave me six months in Riverside Hospital for addict kids.

In retrospect, I think most of my antisocial behavior was due to the fact that I wanted to get laid. In slums, the romantic and heroic figures are those who can beat the system. Soon as a guy *legitimately* makes money, he moves out of the slums. No movie stars or social leaders there, so the guys that could make it with broads were the ones who had cash and some heroic nondrudge role—the hoodlums. So why dig ditches that don't get you the girls, the attention, or the cash to pay off the cops?

I know Frank Serpico's neighborhood, and those cops have been on the take since I was a kid, a known thing. If you're part of the Irish mob, or the Mafia and you pay, no sweat; if you happen to be a poor black or some dumb Puerto Rican that shoots dope, you go to jail. Elements of the New York Police Department are a central source of heroin in the United States; nobody believes this. The police steal heroin, or buy it, off the Corsicans, who sell it to Italians, who sell it to the blacks, who sell it to the Spanish and other blacks. The whites buy it off the blacks, then go back to their neighborhood and sell it to some teen-ager and *he's* the one that gets arrested, by the same coppers that sold it to him. That's why New York City is in shambles, because they all know they're living in a lunatic asylum. For everything a member of the Mafia does wrong, there's twenty cops in back of him.

That scene in the movie *Serpico*, where the cops hit him with a phone book, they don't do that. What they *do*, and they did it to me, they put the phone book on your head and chain you to these hot water pipes. The handcuffs will heat slowly, and they wrap wet handkerchiefs around your wrists so's you won't get a burn, but you'll feel the pain like boiling water. Then they put the phone book on your head, and beat on the book. This might not kill you but your brains might scramble. And they tell you, "We keep this up another half hour, you're gonna go crazy—you gonna talk, or what?" Only way to beat them at that game is to pretend you're *already* crazy.

Problem with the movie *Serpico*, it only showed one-tenth of reality; it's *ten* times that bad. I used to walk into the station house on Alexander and 38th Street; been pinched there twenty times. Timothy J. Incumbent wants to turn out the vote, pick up his button and his literature, hand it out in front of churches, in saloons, and you'll never get hassled. But anybody handing out any *other* campaign literature, first time some of it hits the pavement, he's arrested for littering. And nobody sneaks around corners for the pay-off—you literally walk into the station house and yell, "Lieutenant O'Hara in? Timothy sent me," and he goes in the back.

Like most slum junkies, John took to armed robbery to feed his habit. Gino Platt remembers, "John got the nickname 'Whitey the Priest' because he'd walk around with a turned-around collar and stick people up, always a very colorful guy." But John never thought of himself as an addict; he was only a guy who liked to shoot up once in a while. His ambition was to become a big-time gangster.

JOHN MAHER: The people I looked up to were Frankie C. head of the boxing racket, and Jimmy Gray, an old safecracker out of Toledo, a little fat, bald Italian, done ten fifteen-to-life bits, a legendary burglar, unusual in that he looked like a typical Italian workman of the husky squat variety; a well-read guy, Hegel and Kierkegaard. I met a lot of Jewish pickpockets later in hospital jails. Until the last fifteen years, most of the expert pickpockets were Jews, it was part of their ghetto culture. Irish and Sicilians are bandits, roam the countryside, it's their tradition, whereas the Jew as an oppressed class is easily identifiable in the ghetto. How much can you steal in a ten-block area? So they become pickpockets, working the crowds that come to fairs and bazaars. Silly to steal from their own people because they'd be ostracized.

These were pros who viewed themselves as businessmen. They'd always send the owner back his wallet, an old tradition. Might keep a passport, something you could sell, but you always return the man's papers. A pro *does* these things; he will not cut a man's pocket with a razor and will put the wallet in the mailbox for the police to return. But nowadays a thief will keep *any*thing.

These old Jewish thieves were Damon Runyon characters—Whitey the Mock, Pincus the Hook. You go stealing with them, you're guaranteed your end, and if you get pinched with them, they keep their mouth shut—the old code, the old romance of the thief. There was Irving the Banker who wore spats and a Homburg, carried a gold-headed cane, and could do almost anything you wanted in crime. Figured out the policy action in his head, didn't need an adding machine. And old Moishe Kapoye, who worked "under an umbrella," that is, under the protection of the law, because he was so fabulous a pickpocket, made so much money at it, he could afford to pay off the cops.

These were the men I respected, who taught me to be a regular guy, or get out of the Neighborhood. I can remember some of the old Italian mob members "explaining" things to me when I got out of line: "We don't *do* this, John." Couple of old Irishmen called me over on the docks one day after we whacked around a guy who welched on a deal. They explained to me in no uncertain terms—I was very young at the time—that this was a workingman with eight children, and if I wanted to be a tough guy and steal, go steal off some rich people uptown. But if I bothered any more honest working people on the docks, this would be viewed, shall we say, with mild disfavor.

One time I knocked off a crap game, and thought my head was going to come off my shoulders because I didn't know the guy running the game was connected. This was in a hotel off Broadway in the 70s; me and a couple fellas stuck them up with a pistol, got a few thousand. Week later, a guy comes up to me and says, "It would be *very wise* for you to go to certain people to convince them you meant no disrespect." One of the guys running the game was paying off the cops; "John—I've heard some funny things. You better go explain that what you did was out of ignorance, and not out of a lack of respect."

A friend of mine who was a dope dealer knocked off a Catholic church for a considerable sum. The collection was *returned*. They took him down in a basement, took off his shoes, and burned the soles of his feet with a hot poker and made him walk home barefoot in the snow. They told him, "You sell dope to nice children instead of bums, and now you steal from the church. Now return the money—you can't afford to have God against you, you got enough troubles with the landlord." The woman that burned his feet was an old Italian grandmother; he sold junk to one of her grandchildren who died from an overdose. It was just a mild object lesson so people would understand that God is not to be fucked with.

CHAPTER TWO

The Jails

*"In the middle of the daily race riot,
it's hard to concentrate on Shakespeare."*

At fourteen, John Maher was sent to Warwick
reform school for armed robbery. In court, when the judge
told him how rough he was, John was surprised.

JOHN MAHER: Coming from a neighborhood riddled with
provincial naïveté, I assumed *everybody* was as rough as me.

Warwick, one of many prep schools for prison, was filled
with lost, tortured slum kids—mainly black, some Spanish—
who were utter social victims, caught in gang wars, boosting
a car to go joy-riding, or smoking pot. Once in every two
hundred, they'd maybe get a would-be professional like me,
a stand-up guy, which the administration hates. Anyone who
says, "I don't wanna go to basket-weaving class this morning,
Buster," is a bad guy. You got to kiss their asses. If you're
clever enough to con them into thinking they're rehabilitat-
ing you, if you give them that ego reinforcement, they let
you go.

After six months they transferred me to Otisville, which
was the worst place I ever was, even though they fed me
better and there was no danger of getting killed, like later on
in regular jails. But they couldn't stand what they called my
attitude, which was that these reform-school clowns were in-

competent assholes who couldn't find a man's job, so they settled for glorified baby-sitter at $75 a week while fancying themselves social heroes like Lincoln Steffens.

They had me cutting lumber, and this one supervisor kept bustin' my hump, and I knew it was only a matter of time before I got in a beef with him, or with one of these lonely kids that butter up to the supe like he's some parent figure. I'm going have to break my shovel over his melon because he's jivin' me, droppin' lugs on me, and whatever dirty jobs come up, I get them. Like, they burned this poison sumac on the job and put me downwind of it, where it gets in your lungs and you start coughing blood. Had to wear a handkerchief over my face. So I hit on this trick to get out of work. I rubbed poison sumac on my feet so's they'd swell up and they couldn't put me on the work gang. Now they *know* I done this to myself, and besides I was always talking escape, so they took me out one day because of my attitude.

It was winter, the snow was up to my knees, they had a guy hold me down, put my feet up in the snow and beat my soles with a rubber truncheon. To this day, I got lumps in the center of my feet. It sounds horrible, but I don't want to engross it. It was terrible only on the *mind* because Otisville was a playpen for kids and I didn't belong there.

What these social workers didn't understand was that if a man went along with their little reform schemes, he could never go back home because nobody in the Neighborhood would ever speak to him again. It was a commonplace social-worker notion that anyone who resisted their personal ego-fix was a bad guy. I was so hostile and angry at this bullshit that it showed in my attitude. Most of these poor kids were eating better than they were on the street, so it was a *lark* to them.

I served my full year-and-a-half term at Otisville. After two months on the street I was busted for narcotics addiction and sent to the Brooklyn House of Detention. I was mad about the bust. I got pinched with half a dozen other junkies who were over eighteen; they were found not guilty because they had a lawyer. I was fifteen and didn't have a lawyer, so the judge says he's going to give me two years of "help" by sending me to the state training school.

This wasn't a bad place, staffed by nice people, but they were Babbitt-decent, geared to deal with a six-year-old mentality when they were handling kids fifteen and sixteen. These low-level intellects couldn't find more lucrative employment, so they fed each others' egos by telling each other the reason they did this work was because they liked children; all bullshit.

I got in a fight there, this guy hit me in the melon with a table leg, so when I get out of the hole with my head stitched up, I have to *get* this punk—can't be going home having somebody hit me and not get him back, because nobody on the street would ever *talk* to me again. So I clobbered him with an ax handle, and it was back to the hole again; seclusion they called it. For two weeks in the hole, I figured I got a reputation, so from then on I played *up* to these assholes, say good things about them in the school essays I had to write, "Supervisor Horseface took us boys on a wonderful camping trip," and three months later I was *out*.

This taught me a great lesson for later life. With this kind of correctional creep, so lonely and hurt because they have failed so long in their job, if you give them the slightest hope that they've helped you, they're so thrilled they let you out of jail. First week you're there, start a big scene and just *waste* somebody, really clobber them. You start out by creating the illusion you're a totally dangerous motherfucker. Then six months later, you're *less* dangerous. After eighteen months somebody says, "What a remarkable transformation in this man!" Anyone stupid enough to think that *anyone's* going to get well under the current correctional system *deserves* to get played with.

Six months after John was out of the state training school
he was caught with a half-ounce of heroin in a shoebox. This
time it was no kiddie farm or reform school, but the big time
—three consecutive years on New York's Rikers Island.

JOHN MAHER: This was the armpit of New York City.
Seldom do you meet a real professional thief, or anyone who
ever made any real money, mainly, the socially deprived, a
place for detaining excess populations who are unemployable.
When I went there in 1957, guys were in for Mickey Mouse
stuff like narcotics, assault while drunk. As a pro, I didn't
view jail as a loner. Jail's like rain to a farmer—just make
sure you don't get too much of it. Jail was a chance, with
little risk, to impress gangsters from the Neighborhood; there
were men in all the New York jails who knew my father and
grandfather. On the street, I had to *work* for a rep, but in
jail I could build it easily, pick up the law from older Neighborhood fellas, names I could use to drop on the outside, like
"You was with Yago," or "You was with Irving the Banker."

In a prison like Rikers it's inevitable that any new prisoner is going to be a target for sexual advances. Only two
ways you can handle this: Either you go along with it and
become somebody's punk in return for his protection against
gang-bang rapes—or you do what I did. First time someone
makes a pass, or even hints at it, you say, "Lissen, *punk*, you
so much as lay a hand on me and I will *kill* you, and when
I get outa here, I'll kill your wife, your mother, your whole
fuckin' family!" and you ain't bullshittin', you *mean* it.

After one week, I slash my wrist, way up high where it
wouldn't bother me, to get in the psychiatric ward where
there's better food and coffee, more privacy, and less night-
time racket. You had access to phones in the doctor's office
or X-ray room to maintain your lines of communication on
the outside. You were near the drugs and medicines and the
only women on Rikers Island, the nurses, some of whom
could occasionally be bought. You weren't shook down as

much, and could buy heroin, coke, booze, morphine, even
pot, although most prison types had no use for it, being
either hypes or lushes.

When my wrist healed I got a job in the psychiatric ward
because I could read, write, and spell correctly. It was the
doctor's or the captain's decision to appoint someone a psychiatric clerk. A good line of shit, and a fifty buck donation
to the "Correctional Officers' Benevolent Association" would
get you the job. The doctors were obvious yo-yos incapable
of private practice, senile clowns, refugees from the University of Hungary, 1911. One of my duties was to walk around
and look at the nuts; the ones who are *really* crazy—hearing
voices and talking to cockroaches—you write "faking" on
their report so they'll send them back to the yard to make
room for a prisoner *sane* enough, who can pay us $50 or $100
for the cell. You wouldn't have to pay nothing if you were a
good fellow, and connected, with a mob, a man with "respect" who had kept his mouth shut. So the *real* nuts with
no money or connections never see the inside of the psychiatric ward, except for the few minutes when we transfer
them to Bellevue or Matteawan.

The function of the prison psychiatric ward is to provide
a place where the sane people could go to get away from the
nuts. Nobody believes you when you tell them this.

We got one guy in, a Washington big shot arrested for
drunk driving. This poor, fool gentleman looking like Greg-
ory Peck, he *demanded* to call his wife, so naturally the cops
just punched the holy living shit out of him. We look him
over, "You gonna be in prison only ten days? You wanna be
in the hospital?" We bill him $1,000. On the other hand,
some nice old Jew from downtown, or an Irishman from the
docks who was a regular, we'd get him in for nothing—a socialist experiment.

At night I walked around the tiers reserved for the ones
who were so crazy you couldn't pretend they were faking—

the ones banging their heads on the wall—and try to calm them down. What the doctor tells you to do is Mickey Mouse stuff. You got to realize that in prison, nobody works; the guards just sit around. Once in a while some bright-eyed fool runs in bushy-tailed from the Columbia School of Social Work and wants to change things; he ends up bitter, rotten, and corrupt. If they're snivelers, they go around whining how evil the world is; if they're *mensches*, they take it for what it is and do what good they can.

One day this brand new Ph.D comes around looking for a quorum for his group therapy sessions, so I tell him, "You get us some good coffee and keep my boys out of the hole and we'll go to therapy." I line up this motley crew to sit around in a room while this dopey doctor asks some guy from East Harlem, for Chrissake, how he feels about his *mother!* Well, you don't ask that to *Italians*—they'd just punch the shit out of you—kiddie stuff, you lead the sucker along: "Gee, Doc, I get these terrible feelings of insecurity when I go look for a job." *What* job? When we get out, we don't go for no *job*—we go out and get a *fix*. I've been group therapized thousands of times—it's about as good as exorcism.

Another dodge we used was claiming to be Jews because Hebrew Relief brought us socks, warm clothing, for which we would have to attend services. It was pretty weird, seeing these Chicanos and Irish sitting in chapel, all wearing *yarmulkas* and chanting "shma Yisroel," but there was one thing the rabbi kept saying that all of us snapped to: "Next year we meet in Jerusalem." We knew that Jerusalem meant freedom. It made quite an impression, because to this day I always observe the Jewish holidays, especially Passover whose Seder supper ritual, celebrating the release from bondage, packs an emotional wallop for any oppressed class or race.

You learn very early in Rikers Island that the warden and the guards don't really run the prison. Since prior to the turn

of the century, when the prison was on Blackwell's Island,
the City of New York Department of Corrections personnel,
including the wardens, come from the same blocks as the
prisoners; they just found a less dangerous way of making a
living. How's an Irish prison guard from 10th Avenue going
to go back in his neighborhood saloon if he doesn't take care
of the Irish in prison? How can a black cop go back to his
Harlem apartment unless he takes care of some black guys
who have something to say in his neighborhood? Of course
there's money bribery on the highest levels, but most of it is
emotional bribery. Once I heard a guy in prison tell the
deputy warden, "Lissen, Buster, you might be the boss in
here, but I'm the boss outside, and you gonna live longer
outside than I'm gonnna live in here." The message was *very*
clear. The thieves and crazy people run the streets of New
York; the police have the illusion that they run them, and
the churches share this fantasy.

In prison, the administration is afraid of the correctional
officers, the psychiatric staff, social and medical staff. In turn,
the medical staff despises the social staff who view themselves as Oxford dons, men of exceptional brilliance and talent, forced because of their love of humanity to mingle with
the other scum. The only ones who did some good were your
basic correctional officers who had the job because they had
kids to feed, did not take themselves all that seriously, and
had been through the mill. I never met any city appointee
in the administration worth half a fuck.

Part of my job was to segregate black and white prisoners
in the ward. Prisons reflect American social conditions. The
blacks were tortured, bullied, living with rats, so they're liable
to put a shiv in the nearest white back that symbolizes their
problem. And the whites have the common complaint that
the reformers concentrate almost exclusively on the blacks
and ignore the whites. The administration at all times en-
courages racism, even to the point of pitting white guards

against black guards. I've seen riots in jails where the black guards managed the black team and the white guards were the Vince Lombardis of the white team. In a jungle like that, where dozens of knifings are committed every year, prisoners gravitate toward those most like themselves for mutual protection. In prison, the education system has nothing to do with training prisoners, but it has everything to do with upping the budget and employing a few excess middle-class teachers. In the middle of the daily race riot, it's hard to concentrate on Shakespeare. But of course in those days I was too crazy to perceive such things. I was too busy wanting to grow up to be a big-time gangster.

But all the gangsters I'm trying to impress got no use for junkies, can't trust them, and I'm stickin' up too many people to support the habit and have to go to the slammer for too many years. So I come out of Rikers Island at age twenty-two, determined to kick my habit.

I was ready for a change. In the late fifties, a new consciousness was coming on the country that even began to affect hoodlums like me. My illusions about the romance of the old criminal life were disappearing, and a lot of the old established rackets were being killed off by the technology. The pickpocket was replaced by the purse-snatcher, the sporting girl by the flat-footed streetwalker, the bank robber by the grocery-store holdup man, the safecracker by the automobile breaker-inner. I was on the tail end of a romantic dream, the Golden Age of Crime was over, killed by the two-way radio, flash fingerprints on computer indexing. Urban change destroyed the old criminal life. Once it was hard for a police informer to go back to his old neighborhood, but it was no problem for all these new transients. And in the post-World War II boom, it was possible for racketeers to get ahead *legitimately*—like Agnew.

Housing projects wiped out systems of credit in small family-owned groceries and saloons. The migration of blacks created a polarity, and nobody wanted to spend five years learning to pop a safe, blow a door, or work a burglar-alarm system. People don't want to play cards in back rooms when they can go to Las Vegas. The Vegas mobility destroyed the old family solidarity, like in *The Godfather* when the Mafia chief tells his Vegas-corrupted brother, "You're my brother, and I love you—but don't *ever* take anyone's side against the Family again."

There had to be some other life for me to build. Obviously I had fucked up my life pretty bad, because according to the old code, a good thief doesn't use drugs, doesn't steal from poor people—which I did all the time—so I hadn't even lived up to the standards acceptable in *that* culture. In my provincial stupidity, I thought if I kicked drugs I could get a *legitimate* job—like in the numbers, a bookmaker or a shylock. So I had no real reasons for kicking my habit when I got into Synanon, and how I got in was a very weird story.

I was sticking up a junk connection in broad daylight on the corner of 8oth and Amsterdam, and trying to get off the block before I get mobbed either by the cops or the connection's friends, and I don't want to be killing anybody with that many witnesses around. So as I'm easing off this corner like Billy the Kid, this guy drives by I did a favor for in the penitentiary, Dr. Richard Korn, a psychiatrist who asked me to round up some of the boys for group therapy so's he could get his grant, and in turn, act as our rabbi, get us Italian coffee. He honks at me while I'm backing off the street, opens the door, pulls me in, drives me to the Institute of Psychodrama, where they ask me, "How would you like to go to Synanon in Santa Monica, California, and kick your habit?" Now this shrink was very smart—he kept me doped up all night, because as long as you're loaded you tell yourself, "Yeah, I wanna be *cured*."

In the morning, the Doc drives me to his bank to pick up my plane fare and leaves me waiting outside. I'm nodding out, acting like a general asshole, when the Burglary Squad drives up and sees me with my black fedora and the eye patch where I got my face busted the week before. They surround me:

"Whud you doin' outside this bank at nine in the morning? Makin' a deposit? This is highly doubtful." Fortunately, the Doc comes out and they ask him, "You with this bum? What's happenin'?"

"I'm sending him to California to kick his habit." The Burglary Squad then personally escorts me to the airport, which they do with any known pro—if you can pick a lock or use a torch, they'll do *anything* to get you out of town. They put me on the plane with a note pinned to my coat, "Deliver to Synanon." I go into the plane's john to take a fix, and overdosed. They carried me off the plane in Santa Monica and deposited me on Synanon's doorstep like an infant in swaddling clothes.

When I come to, I'm lying on this couch in the middle of Synanon's living room, sicker than a dog, no money, no familiar Neighborhood face to help me score, when this big, fat guy, ugly beyond belief, sits down on my couch while I'm throwin' up, and with this voice like a concrete mixer, growls, "Sonny, if you're sick and think you're going to die, we'll get you a doctor. But if you *don't* die, and bug our doctor, we're going to be *very angry* with you!"

This was the kind of attitude Chuck Dederich slowly forced on me during the next eight years—the responsibility to kick the habit *myself*. Not, "We're going to help you, Junior," but "Why don't you help yourself? Here're the tools!"

CHAPTER THREE

The Old Man

*"You're going to have more fun than
you ever had in your life."*

In the mid-fifties, while the teen-age John
Maher was scoring for heroin in the South Bronx, Charles E.
"Chuck" Dederich stumbled along the beaches of Santa
Monica, a hopeless drunk at forty. Booze had made a mess of
his college career at Notre Dame, his many marriages, his executive posts with Gulf Oil and Douglas Aircraft where his
natural bent for leadership and grasp of corporate structure
had marked him for an early and spectacular rise.

Alcoholics Anonymous (AA) helped Dederich get off the
"smart juice," as they had millions of others, with a revolutionary method of freeing the addictive personality—the dis-
covery that ex-patients make the best doctors. (On a recent
TV panel of AA members, a young woman who had been
alcoholic since fifteen said, "When the family told me, I
turned off. When the priest told me, I thought, 'What does
he know?' When the doctor told me, I didn't hear. But when
a room full of alkies who had been through the same kind of
hell, and worse, told me, "You're an alcoholic," there was
just no way I could kid myself any longer.")

Once Dederich kicked the booze he became a commanding force that AA had to reckon with. They sent him around

the country as their prize lecturer and fund-raiser in a presentable suit borrowed from a fellow member.

When Dederich entered a room, he took immediate charge. Even in quiet repose, his presence was so ominous, even frightening, that no one could take their eyes off him. He was built like a Japanese wrestler with stubby legs that seemed too short for his concrete-block torso topped by a massive, lopsided head. People were hypnotized by the rumbling voice, the contagious laughter, the withering sarcasm. A tough corporation head who never cut loose his earthy roots, Dederich mixed Plato and Emerson with gutter obscenities and down-home wit. He gave off the aura of an honest man, desperately concerned with the fate of his fellows.

Dederich functioned as a priest-confessor for a dozen AA members who shared his passion for "talking philosophy" and his boredom with AA's God-directed rhetoric. He was living on unemployment benefits in a tiny Ocean Beach flat that became a Wednesday night clubhouse and discussion group.

One night a member brought a friend who was not a lush, but a heroin addict, in the hope that Dederich could straighten him out. Dederich neither knew nor cared that medical science, psychotherapy, and government experts had long written off heroin addiction as a terminal illness. Here was just another character-disordered individual, one more person with problems who might be helped to help himself.

More addicts, men and women, black and white, started to rent flats close to Dederich's seedy clubhouse to take part in the much-talked-of attack therapy sessions called synanons, after some junkie's attempt to pronounce a mixture of seminars and symposiums.

AA was not big enough to contain Dederich, who dreamed of an inner-directed community that would go far beyond AA's limited and God-oriented views. If AA could get people off booze, maybe he could get them doing other things. He began to envision a self-contained group of former addicts that could alter the life-style of millions and make a positive revolutionary thrust in crisis-ridden America.

The showdown came with AA when they demanded the purge of all drug addicts. Dederich responded by tossing out all the alcoholics, save himself, and forming his own group of ex-junkies.

Dederich conceived Synanon as a result of two dramatic events: An intake of LSD under controlled hospital conditions induced a state he found akin to delerium tremens, but provided insights into the form Synanon was to assume. (A few months later he repeated the experiment, but "absolutely nothing happened." This was the last time he used any mind-altering substance.) The second, and most important catalyst in the founding of Synanon, was his chance reading of Emerson's essay "Self-Reliance" which became the new organization's catechism and creed:

There comes a time in everyone's life when he arrives at the conviction that envy is ignorance; that imitation is suicide; that he must accept himself for better or for worse as is his portion; that though the wide universe is full of good, no kernel of nourishing corn can come to him but through his toil bestowed on that plot of ground which is given to him to till. The power which resides in him is new in nature, and none but he knows what it is that he can do, nor does he know until he has tried. Bravely let him speak the utmost syllable of his conviction. God will not have his work made manifest by cowards.

A man is relieved and gay when he has put his heart into his work and done his best; but what he has said or done otherwise shall give him no peace. As long as he willingly accepts himself, he will continue to grow and develop his potentialities. As long as he does not accept himself, much of his energies will be used to defend rather than to explore and actualize himself.

No one can force a person toward permanent and creative learning. He will learn only if he *wills* to. Any other type of learning is temporary and inconsistent with the self and will disappear as soon as the threat is removed. Learning is possible in an environment that provides information, the setting, materials, resources and by his being there. God helps those who help themselves.

For Dederich, "Self-Reliance" was not an idle literary essay, but a "personal letter addressed directly to me, a manual of directions, essential for the running, operation, and maintenance of the human psyche."

With his $33 unemployment check, Dederich incorporated Synanon in September 1958 in a rented Ocean Park storefront with a few dozen addicts "in a live-in situation with family characteristics, emphasizing self-reliance rather than dependence on a higher being." It was financially rough on the burgeoning new family, dependent entirely on Chuck's unemployment benefits. A motherly soul with a psychoanalytic background moved in, did the cooking, and threw her pension check into the kitty. Some older hypes were put to work hustling stale sandwiches and day-old doughnuts from bakery trucks. Dederich would wander about, telling the small group in a voice that rang with absolute conviction, "Stick around. Something very big is happening here. Something important. You're going to have more fun than you ever had in your life. You'll be amazed where this thing is going to lead, what consequences it will have, not just for us, but for this entire crazy country of ours. It will emerge."

Early Synanon residents went into immediate father-transference on exposure to Dederich, who assumed complete control of the household. He knew that junkies were emotional infants with disastrous family histories. Old World discipline had been destroyed by the newly mobile American society with its ghettos, urban squalor, welfare system, and ultrapermissive child rearing fashionable among the educated class. No one had told the addict, "Don't touch the stove—it burns; don't run out in the street—you'll get hit." Dederich treated addicts like small children until he was satisfied they could think and function like reasoning adults. A man who

threatened violence would have his head shaved and wear a
sign, "I'm a little boy—please laugh at my idiot attempts to
act tough." A woman caught using cough syrup for a cheap
high would wear a stocking cap and be deprived the use of
make-up. Infractions would be met by one of Dederich's horrendous verbal flayings, or haircuts, "guaranteed," in the
words of one recipient, "to skin the hide off a razorback hog."
Many couldn't take it, and split. Those who remained developed strong bonds to the group and idolatrous loyalty to
its leader.

Incoming addicts kicked their habit on Synanon's living
room couch, in full view of the family, with few of the over-
publicized movie terrors of isolated, wall-climbing with-
drawal in some skid-row hotel. Comely young women fed
them chicken soup and urged them to "hang tough—I was
a boss, hope-to-die dope fiend six months ago, and if I can
kick, anybody with your Mickey Mouse, peewillie habit can
kick too." Dederich would amble over to the shivering,
blanket-covered addict to snort, "You still here? Hell, I
thought you'd have hightailed it out of here long before
now!" Proving to the Old Man they could stick it became
important.

Once off the "kicking couch," addicts were put to work,
often for the first time. There were toilets to swab, floors to
clean, food to cook, and when the organization and its mem-
bership grew, letters to write, cars to repair, commissaries to
build. People whose only contact had been with fellow addicts were stationed at the front door to greet the press, parole
officers, and other squares curious about this new outfit that
was beginning to attract publicity. "Hello, my name is
Booker T. Jones. Is this your first visit? Let me show you
around, answer your questions . . ."

Dederich read Emerson aloud to the group. Semiliterate
junkies whose vocabularies had been limited to "fix," "hype,"

and "skin-pop" were up all night arguing about Plato's allegory of the cave, or what Emerson meant by "imitation is suicide."

The main re-educative tool was the attack-therapy session, the synanons that Dederich later christened the Game. His theory was that since games were fun, games about people should be more fun than whacking little balls around. The purpose of the Game was to develop psychic muscles and human insight, and since laughter, tears, rage, and love are the most basic emotions, he counted no Game "worth diddly-shit unless every player is either screaming with laughter, bawling like a child, hugging each other—or on the verge of physical violence."

Dederich developed the Game when encounter group therapy was beginning to supplant one-to-one psychotherapy in America, and he took pains to reorient newcomers who had undergone psychiatric treatment. "We're not interested if you wet the bed at ten, or if your scoutmaster jacked you off—we want to know what you did today, and what motions you're going through to improve your behavior tomorrow." As a result, Dederich claimed he saw people go through amazing transformations; whores became madonnas, pimps turned into leaders of men. He encouraged obscene and hysterical outpourings in Games to get bottled-up feelings of hostility out in the open. His own prowess in Games was legendary. An aggressive Hunter College social worker was bold enough to put the Game on Dederich, indicting him as a supersquare, a philistine who thought music and the arts mere toys to distract lesser folk from more pressing social concerns. It took him all of fifteen minutes to thrust her back to yowling infancy, and another ten minutes to patch her up.

As Game players grew in toughness and skill, he urged them into Dissipations—marathon thirty- to forty-eight-hour Games, believing that people "dissipate their psychic energies in dreams," and that with no sleep to act as a protective shield, players were put through "fantastic changes—they stopped conning us and experienced some real breakthroughs."

Synanon as a group had its own breakthrough on a June night in 1959, the Night of the Big Cop Out. While some residents had been living clean, many clung to the old street ways, hoarding a stash of pot, bennies, or even shaving lotion, anything to get high. Most of Synanon's law-abiders knew, but true to the old criminal code, they never told Dederich. Squealing on your friends was still the unthinkable crime. This changed overnight when a resident in a Game accused his best friend of using. "Look, shit-head, I know you got loaded last week because we got loaded together!" Suddenly the urge to cop out, to admit using drugs and to finger known users, swept the clubhouse. Dederich roused all from bed at 3:00 A.M. to join in an orgy of self-confession, obscene accusations, howls of denial, and maniacal laughter. He climaxed the meeting with a still-talked-about marathon speech, proclaiming that the Code of the Street had been replaced by the Synanon Ethic. Loyalty to the group now transcended the outmoded criminal taboo against squealing. "We had finally emerged as a family."

Living on land condemned by the State of California, the family was ordered out of Ocean Park to make room for a parking lot. This ouster was no tragedy for Dederich. He had been planning a move away from the slums to a class neighborhood where addicts would not be thrown back into the environment that spawned their problem. Thanks to the inspired wheeling and dealing at which Dederich and his staff had grown adept, Synanon's fifty residents moved into the former headquarters of the National Guard in Santa Monica's exclusive beach front. A group of Synanon's new-found square backers with top Beverly Hills connections assumed responsibility for the two-year lease.

The move to Santa Monica marked a dramatic turn-around. This archconservative haven of the wealthy-retired, aghast at the invasion of interracial ex-cons, immediately countered with a frenzied campaign of harrassment. The Santa Monica Evening Outlook ran daily editorials demanding the removal of "Sin Anonymous." An endless parade of health, fire, and building inspectors tramped through the premises, citing dozens of infractions that would require a fortune to correct. Inflamed by the sight of Dederich's black wife Bettye, a former addict and prostitute, the John Birch Society organized meetings, denouncing Synanon as a free-love center. A local judge ordered them to vacate on the grounds that Dederich was operating a hospital in a non-hospital zone. When he refused, Dederich became the first, and perhaps the only, citizen of the United States to be sent to jail—twenty-five days—for a residential zoning violation.

Santa Monica's all-out war had the same result as censoring a movie or book—it attracted overnight publicity and support. Synanon polarized the Southern California community. Judges, movie stars, sociologists, real-estate dealers, business executives, and lawyers came to see what kicked up all the fuss, liked what they saw, and donated money, goods, and services. Some even moved in as residents. The mass media began to take notice of a colorful new method of treating addiction. Favorable pieces ran in Time magazine and the liberal weeklies. Dentists and doctors set up free clinics, grocers gave canned goods, housewives unloaded old furniture.

In 1967, the nine-year-old Foundation purchased Santa Monica's palatial and long-empty Del Mar Club, valued at $3.5 million. When Dederich moved his growing band into this fancy beach-front hotel with its Olympic-size pool, tennis courts, and steam baths, a private contractor invaded the property with bulldozers, destroying fences and beach houses. When Synanon members protested, a specially assigned task force of thirty police threw them bodily into patrol wagons. Banner front-page headlines and photos of this bizarre melee multiplied national support. Lawyers volunteered legal aid and Mayor Sam Yorty invited Synanon to move to nearby Los Angeles.

Branches opened in New York, Detroit, San Diego, and San Francisco's plush residential area, Pacific Heights, where the pattern of harrassment by citizens' groups, neighborhood improvement associations, City Hall, health, fire, and building inspectors was repeated, with the expected publicity. To thwart an attempted ouster from San Francisco's Clay Street mansion via a zoning law restricting houses in this area to single-family dwellings, Mr. and Mrs. Dederich registered as the single family, listing the other residents as servants, whose numbers were not restricted by law. The right-wing press pictured Dederich as an Indian pasha attended by a bevy of butlers, maids, cooks, footmen, and masseurs.

Synanon expanded its self-fueling empire, running gas stations, selling office supplies and raffle tickets, buying up prime real estate, like the Olympic Hotel in Oakland and the magnificently rural Marconi Hotel overlooking California's Tomales Bay. Well-meaning friends tried to interest the federal government and large foundations in coming through with subsidies, but after repeated bouts with Washington bureaucrats, Dederich turned down over $1 million in grants. There was always some string attached, like the "pee-in-the-bottle" program. (In return for funds from the National Institute of Mental Health, all Synanon residents would be given a monthly urinalysis to prove they were drug-free.) Dederich would have none of it, "We've got something better than piss—something we call trust." Rebuffed, the government subsidized other groups to "start something just like Synanon" in New York and Detroit. "These government-funded, slum-located copies," insisted Dederich, "were always total failures."

Synanon was getting on without government money. Hundreds of squares, some rich and influential, flocked to Synanon as a new-style church and home-away-from-home, especially when Dederich opened the Game Club to nonaddicts. He felt that if Games could straighten out dope friends, convicts, and blacks—the most alienated and encapsulated elements of society—then the Game should work for anybody. Celebrities, lawyers, students, longshoremen, and middle-class couples addicted to nothing stronger than coffee were standing in line to play the wild and dirty Synanon Game, eager to get their egos bruised by pimps, whores, and junkies, and maybe to get the chance to give as good as they got. Dederich charged Game Club members one penny a month dues, and the waiting list grew into the hundreds, with special Games for teen-agers, divorced women, blacks ("suedes"), married couples, and "high-ego" Games for the rich and famous.

As the Square Game Club grew, Dederich looked for someone to head the San Francisco Chapter who could relate to intellectuals, a crack Game player, charismatic, a wit. He settled on John Maher.

CHAPTER FOUR

The Undergraduate

"Dederich impressed me because he took no money."

Five years earlier, in the summer of 1962, John Maher was kicking his habit on Synanon's living room couch, looking for ways to score. With all these junkies around, somebody must be holding. But for the first time, he found himself in an alien land. On the street or in jail, there was always some old hype buddy with a spare cap of heroin. Now he was three thousand miles from home, surrounded by strangers.

JOHN MAHER: My immediate tribal reaction was, "These people are not from my Neighborhood—they can mean me nothing but harm. I'll lay up here a while, get my health back, and then go back on the grift [the old street life]." This was a different breed of addicts and thieves than I had been reared with, except for a few old-timers like Charlie Hamer who knew what San Francisco was like in the old Damon Runyon days. Their concept of drugs was, the youth authority locks you up and then Mommy drives from Pasadena to bail you out. There were no Neighborhood people, they were California-soft, there was no *style* to them, and while some of them were bright, they were completely untrustworthy because they reeked of weakness.

I tried to impress these weaklings by acting tough, but

instead of getting mad, Dederich and his buddies would whoop with laughter and say with great pity, "This poor child is deranged." For me, this was a whole new situation, like in those old movies where they catch a primitive man from New Guinea and take him to the city, where he relates by snatching a chicken off a plate, and they respond by smiling benevolently. This broke down all the garbage in me, because if they reacted with counterviolence or nonsense, it would have reinforced the silly position I was in. Synanon was an easier way of getting smarter, of getting my emotional needs satisfied for the *right* reasons, rather than the false reasons of image.

Soon, I knew there was something here I could benefit from, not in terms of curing my habit, because I never thought of myself as an addict—I was a guy who liked to shoot up and could stop whenever I wanted. But it was obvious to me that I needed a break from the New York scene, and there was something here for me to learn.

Dederich impressed me because he took no money. I never met anyone before who would help you for no money or salary. It reeked out of the man that he didn't have a racket, he was basically honest and had some interesting concepts. And I knew my life was not producing the quality that it should. Dederich put the responsibility on *me*, "Sonny, why don't you kick your habit?" Prior to this, either the right-wing nuts clobber your head, or the left-wing nuts kiss your ass, until you're bananas. In hospitals, little old Red Cross ladies cried a lot and told me what a hard life I had, or in jail, guards would beat me and scream what a dirty sonofabitch I was. So Dederich made sense and became a father figure to me.

CHUCK DEDERICH: I suppose I was the first successful person John ever ran into, successful in the legitimate sense. I was someone he could role model to, whose good will he wanted. For the first time, he found somebody he wanted something more from than money. John came in here with all the things wrong with him that you get in young street addicts who spent most of their teen-age years in kiddie joints and jails—no manners, morals, or integrity. He was suspicous, paranoid, a cornered animal, wrote crazy letters to nonexistent people. After a while, it became apparent that he was kind of bright, a genuine Synanon miracle.

Dederich urged Maher to read Emerson, Buckminster Fuller, Dr. Abraham Maslow, and they would argue. In Synanon's early years, Dederich still had time for these bull sessions.

JOHN MAHER: Emerson, like all the New England transcendentalists, had a pragmatic view of the world, tinged with the mysticism and romantics of Christianity, a rather nice and stabilizing view. But like Bucky Fuller and Alan Watts, Emerson is what I call a soft thinker, full of pleasant and vague concepts of flowing, groovy oneness. I veered more to the hard thinkers like Marx and Freud who lay out basic postures and directions, something you can *argue* about. More important was what I got from Dederich—the need to adopt the 100 percent moral position. When he came out with these maddening old bromides like "Honesty is the best policy," and "Confession is good for the soul," it wasn't some bullshit Methodist sermon—these were concepts the man *lived* by, and they meant something. He taught me never to do anything I would be ashamed to read on the front page of a newspaper.

Synanon put Maher to work cleaning toilets, but he soon angled a kitchen job making coffee, giving him time to rap with the crew, and take stock of the strength and weakness of the organization and its people.

JOHN MAHER: After eight months of making coffee, one day I went downstairs and announced to the group, "Dederich told me to build a commissary." I collected all the canned goods, tools, bedding, and clothes, built a little shed, and become the central disbursement unit for all Foundation supplies.

They never found out that Dederich never gave the order. In a straight dictatorship like Synanon, nobody dreamed that anyone would dare use the name of the leader in vain. This was only the first of many times I used this technique. Whenever I wanted something done I'd say, "Der Führer told me to do this." They'd suspect me, but were too terrified to check with Dederich, and besides I was bustin' my hump, working twelve hours a day to provide a service that became indispensable.

I moved out of the commissary by selling them the idea of raising funds by putting on a big art show on the UCLA campus. This went over big, so they transferred me to the San Diego branch to start Synanon Industries, organizing an advertising specialties business, hustling imprinted ball-point pens and office supplies to small firms and large corporations, training a sales force by taking advantage of the natural gift of the addict—the ability to bullshit.

His next move was to San Francisco's Seawall, a sprawling waterfront warehouse leased by Synanon as dining room, social center, and Game Club. He organized the annual Synanon Street Fair, a colorful front-page event with its lavish array of arts and crafts, refreshment booths, sports car raffles, and games of chance.

Dederich picked Maher to head Seawall's mushrooming Game Club whose fifteen hundred members included the co-inventor of the Polaroid Land Camera and a leading Bay Area conservationist, a millionaire real-estate developer, a black community leader who was head of the University of California Dental School, the city's highest-paid disc jockey. They began to prize a Game with John. For five years he had sharpened his verbal-combative skills and his capacity for ruthless self-examination. His gut-level encounters with the top echelons of society formed his postgraduate course. It was easier for him to operate around City Hall, since he had more mobility and muscle than in prison, his Marine boot camp for invading the establishment. It was like converting from wartime to peacetime. After eight years in Synanon, he was ready to move out.

JOHN MAHER: I hadn't been in Synanon six months before I realized that most of the people there weren't nearly as bright as everyone said, but were dependent idiots. But it was a necessary phase of growth to have them believe themselves to be creative and imaginative social planners, so I went along with the party line. One of the problems of curing addicts is that their ego has been deflated, and a trick to get them back on their feet, and keep them clean long enough to re-educate them, is to forcefully inflate their ego. The slightest accomplishment must get massive approval from the group, like a bunch of Hadassah ladies oohing and aahing over "little Sylvia Horowitz, who will probably grow up to win the Nobel Prize—did you ever taste little Sylvia's cookies?" So when little Sylvia goes out into the world to discover nobody gives a fuck about her, or her cookies, her ego is so rapidly deflated she feels acute pain. Now, the smarter people in Synanon sensed this ego inflation was artificial. As a director of the Foundation, I could go to the president of most banks and get an appointment, or crash a senator's office because he's never sure how many votes I represent. Looking back on it, it sounds crazy. Here I am, out of prison less than a year, never having a successful marriage, never propagating my own kind, poorly educated except for the reading I could do in jail—and people would ask me to address huge college rallies while the mob cheers, "Right on!"

Any independent thinker like me who goes into a place like Synanon, where egos are artificially inflated by the social device of setting one up as intelligent by virtue of one's lifestyle, is a threat if he offers an equally valid, but *alternative* life-style; so the group brings heavy pressure to make you conform. In Games, people would attack me for "obscurantism" because I thought many of them rigid and silly in their views. Since I tend to talk in *non sequiturs*, it drove them bananas because it didn't fit into their pattern of total conformity. Just like in reform school, where they said my attitude was wrong, Dederich would counter by giving me another marathon chewing-out, a verbal haircut. When you have a society like Synanon in which the ultimate virtue is obedience, and the unconscious gut of the group is not loose and diverse, they want to equalize everybody so they don't feel left out. The mob unconsciously tries to prevent those unique and brilliant talents within the group from doing their *schtick*.

Just as Dederich, when in AA, conceived a better way of treating the addictive personality, I began to think of a logical extension of Synanon. The three organizations that have cured more drug addicts are, in order, Red China, the Black Muslims, and Synanon. But they have done so only at the tremendous cost of imposing total conformity. There began to take shape in my mind an organization that would represent an enormous step forward in the social evolutionary process—a group that could cure addicts by tolerating diversity, and get these social victims back in society as productive members.

From the time Dederich got my head on straight, I hoped Synanon would become something else. I was far more impressed with its potential than with its reality. Dederich was quickly abandoning his early revolutionary position to retreat into an isolation that was Amish in its totality. He began to adopt the notion that since the world outside is crazed beyond redemption, you build a remote and alternative community, pool everyone's money, goods, and services, and move in for the rest of your life. Over the years,

Dederich had changed from a preacher of social revolution to a preacher of social containment.

I didn't see this as feasible, since we are utterly dependent upon the mainstream of the economy and the laws. I thought the way to survive was to build a strong economic base to endure the stress of the twentieth century, and to ally ourselves with other people of good will—the Farm Workers Union, Chicano groups, Prisoners' Union, peace movement, women's lib, gay lib, the responsive people working within our two major political parties, and the other potent social movements that were mushrooming in the sixties. Synanon never had any contact with these groups, or even a rudimentary working knowledge of this social upheaval going on around them.

Synanon was making the mistakes most pioneers make. I wanted to build on these mistakes that were inherent in Dederich's education—a Jesuit who spent his years working as a corporation man for Gulf Oil. Within the framework of the corporate view, he's a brilliant man, but outside that framework, very naïve. In the process of re-educating his people, to protect himself against the endless demands of his patients, Dederich developed a defense against being drained to death that made him as isolated as Nixon, not in his philosophy, but in the way he became a loner, with no one to counterbalance his massive ego. One of his tricks, if he was afraid you'd do something without him, or differ with him, no matter how trivial, was to bring immediate heat. He could never delegate authority. His underlings worked hard, but Dederich retained all control, and was whimsical about its use. One day he'd come in and say, "That's *great* what you're doing!" Next day he'd stroll in dead pan and say, "We've *always* been against that." This was his fun, but it's not the way you get adults to cooperate, so the brightest people in the group started moving out, leaving him with a bunch of ass-kissing sychophants who couldn't run a tenement without him.

The Synanon squares began to leave in droves, many of them turned up later in Delancey Street. Synanon made the mistake of developing the worst of its people in Square Game Clubs, rather than the most charming, the brightest, and the most fun. Their wrong theory was, the more time you spent in the Game Club, helping out, the better person you were. They didn't realize Bertrand Russell didn't have three weekends a month he could devote to helping dope fiends, so the Game Club was taken over by endless hoards of fat ladies and lonely lawyers who were bored with their wives and had plenty of time in the evening because nobody wanted to hang out with them.

Synanon had become a very boring place. Square Games, which used to be more fun than the Marx brothers, took on grim overtones as they began to stress total fealty to the Foundation. Instead of indicting a Game player for not finishing the novel, or cheating on his wife, the group would attack him on Mickey Mouse issues, like not buying gas at a Synanon station. A big real-estate man who spent untold hours lining up shrewd land deals for Synanon, finally split after relentless Game pressure to donate his fat bank balance to the Foundation and move in as a resident. They badgered a prominent rancher without mercy to bequeath his extensive land holdings to Synanon, until he left.

By 1968 the number of splitees reached alarming proportions. Synanon responded with a desperate attempt to wring a committment from its people by shaving all the men's heads, even the squares, many of whom were in the public eye. (In February 1975, Synanon's women voluntarily shaved their heads, as did the men, as an expression of group committment and loyalty.) Dederich had little to do with this, since he was busy with his new facility at Tomales Bay, leaving an insecure and fanatical band of carbon copies to drive out the brightest people we had. Synanon took on all the trappings of a Benedictine cloister. In the early days, Dederich was proud of his graduates—reformed addicts who could live clean and function on the outside: Zev Putterman, a top producer for PBS televsion; Jack Ross, formerly "Jake the Snake," with Doubleday publishers in New York; poll-winning musicians Charlie Haden, Esther Phillips, and Joe Pass. But all this changed as tremendous heat was put on those who made noises about leaving the monastary. Dederich said, "Why should I take in some sabertooth animal off the street, spend five years cleaning him up, capping his teeth, and then lose him to Standard Oil when Synanon has its *own* gas stations to run?" This was a valid argument for Synanon, but it didn't take me where I wanted to be. You can't build a successful social movement without any contact with society. Like the Catholic church, you need graduates to go out into the field and proselytize to keep the movement growing.

To learn to cope with the outside world, I started going to night school in Oakland. Synanon busted me from assistant director to dishwasher. I'd saved some money and planned to vacation in Guatamala; they reacted like I wanted to set up a whorehouse in the main lounge: "You must be totally insane—why would anybody want to go to Guatemala when he could vacation at our facility in Tomales Bay?"

The final break came over Maher's intention to divorce Betty, his wife of four years, a former addict who met him while they were living in the Santa Monica house.

JOHN MAHER: Betty and I got married under unusual circumstances. A lot of couples like us were living together, and the Santa Monica police were going to enforce some medieval laws on the books against fornication and living out of wedlock. So Dederich ordered everyone who was shacking up to get married one week in 1963. Betty was a good person, and I admired her, but she wasn't the one I wanted to spend the rest of my life with and obviously she felt the same way. Synanon's position was that I should patch up the marriage. I said this was ridiculous.

DAN GARRETT (head of Synanon's legal department and Dederich's second in command): I summoned John one morning and told him he was being transferred to Santa Monica on a one o'clock bus that afternoon. John said, "I'm not leaving," bolted out the door—and that was the last time we ever saw him.

CHAPTER FIVE

The Split

"An extension of my father's house."

JOHN MAHER: When I split from Synanon, I had no idea of starting my own movement. I was like a man trained to live in a company town. What does he do when he goes to New York? I could discuss Emerson and Albee, but didn't know how to get a Social Security card. But in the back of my mind there was the nagging notion that someday I would have to build a Society of Friends that could bypass all the nonsense in our culture.

It all started one day on Polk Street where I was living in a cheap flat, casting about for something to do. Ran into an old Chicano buddy, drunk, punching some people out over Willie Mays's batting average; took him home and put him up for the night. Next day he brings his wife. Then four Synanon splitees heard about where I was living and moved in. Had to look around for more room and found a two-story flat on Bush Street that rented for $300 a month.

I raised the rent money by borrowing from loan sharks, what we call shylocks, who are illegal because they charge usurious interest rates, $6.00 for every $5.00 borrowed, interest payable weekly, and Mafia methods of collecting, like breakage of legs or worse. None of the legit loan companies or banks would touch me with my criminal record, or if they

did, they wanted exorbitant interest. But the shylocks
charged me no interest at all. Why? Because they were the
only money lenders I could find who were interested in helping kids.

Maher at first called the new group *Ellis Island*, after New
York's debarkation point for nineteenth-century immigrants
eager to start life in the New World; but he soon found the
name copyrighted by another corporation. He settled for *Delancey Street*, Manhattan's East Side settlement of Jews,
Irish, and Italians who sewed the cloth, built the subways,
saved their pennies, and sent for their families abroad.

JOHN MAHER: We wanted to get back to the original
concept of a bunch of wild-eyed fanatics who came over
here to build the New Jerusalem and not ask Uncle Nixon
for another handout. We're radicals in Delancey Street because we *work*.

Maher incorporated those concepts that had worked for
Synanon: no drugs or violence, the Game, the need to locate
in rich neighborhoods, a return to the early American work
ethic to end the individual's dependence on welfare, federal
grants, corporate and foundation funds. He rejected the ideas
of Synanon that he felt were proven failures: Synanon had
withdrawn to an isolated, utopian commune that had no
contact with current social movements; Delancey Street
would build a working alliance with hard-hat unions, women's
lib, senior citizens, the Prisoners' Union, the Farm Workers
Union, the Urban League, the antiwar movement, gay lib,
the Black Caucus, and responsive Republicans and Demo-
crats in City Hall, Sacramento, and Congress. Synanon took
no part in politics; Delancey Street's political clubs would get
out the vote for supportive candidates and would lobby to
change laws. Synanon discouraged its people from leaving the
commune to live and work on the outside; Delancey Street
would aim to put the ex-addict back into society as a productive member with strong economic and emotional ties to the

group. Synanon stressed total allegiance to an organization where everyone had to fit in; Delancey Street would encourage a diversity of ideas and life-styles.

JOHN MAHER: Synanon feels the individual is best served by the survival of the community; Delancey Street feels the community is best served by the survival of the individual. If Synanon is the monastic order, Delancey Street is the Masons, and like the Masons, we plan to survive under *any* regime.

Maher courted a working relationship with Synanon to avoid the destructive infighting that plagued so many radical movements in the past.

CHUCK DEDERICH: One time when John needed a favor from a New Yorker who was a long-time Synanon benefactor, he phoned and asked for my blessing because he didn't want me to feel he was hustling one of our contacts. I told him to go right ahead. And when Synanon sued the San Francisco *Examiner* for libel, John called me and asked if he could be a witness, sign a deposition, do anything to help.

JOHN MAHER: Delancey Street is *not* going to fall into that Stalin-Trotsky, splinter group, internecine warfare trap that fucked up the socialist movement after the Bolshevik Revolution. Let's get one thing straight—Synanon does nothing but *good*. Dederich is a genius, the most significant influence on my life. I'm not joining that pack of ingrates that now attacks the Synanon that saved their lives, those endless whiners who couldn't cut the mustard. Synanon certainly beats the role of the divorced woman with two kids who feels worthless, or a lonely guy who messed up four marriages, whose job takes him on the road, and who has no roots. But Synanon is a limiting experience that tends to alienate people of superior intelligence, the kind we want in Delancey because we want to keep getting that feedback. The stew is what you put in the pot, and in most movements, the stew gets weaker because the pot attracts the same kind of meat. We need a diversity of role models for our people to relate to—businessmen and artists, computer experts and history teachers. When you grow up, you leave your father's house and build something of your own that is an extension. Dederich did this when he left AA to found Synanon.

The communal life-style pioneered by Synanon was adapted by the new group, but since Dederich had broken the ice, Delancey Street grew much faster. Maher had built a following in Synanon, whose disaffected squares now flocked to Delancey Street, making it easier to hustle canned goods, sign leases, feed the growing band of residents, and find jobs for them on the outside.

PAT DONNELLY (former addict-convict who knew Maher in Synanon): Those early days in Delancey were hideous, because you didn't know how long the outfit would last. Here I was, kicking in better than $1,000 a month to Delancey—my total salary as service advisor to Lincoln-Mercury —and drawing a few bucks for walking-around money. I'd done this for six months, was out $6,000, and had nothing to show for it. What's more, I didn't let these terrible anxiety feelings out in Games, which is what Games are for, because I was a director and didn't want to scare off the new people. Besides, why should I dump all this trouble on John, who had more than his share? But the turning point came when John moved us out of the Bush Street flat and into the Arabian Consulate in the fanciest part of town. That change, and the publicity and support it attracted, convinced all of us that Delancey Street was out of the woods and here to stay.

With more than a dozen residents crammed into the stolidly middle-class Bush Street apartment, Maher was ready to invade a rich neighborhood, in keeping with the philosophy he picked up from Dederich.

JOHN MAHER: All social problems should move to where

the rich people live. One of the crazy situations in this
country is that rich people's living space is *cheaper* per square
foot than slum warehouse space. For the same money that
would keep fifteen senior citizens or crippled vets in a rat
trap at government expense, they could live in a gorgeous
mansion in the ritziest part of town. But of course rich
people don't want them there, so they keep these halfway
houses in the ghetto where you can't cure addicts, any more
than you can cure an alcoholic in a bar; in the morning
people line up at the welfare office, and at night they line up
to get a fix or buy a whore. You've got to bring these problems to the people with money, expertise, and the political
clout to *do* something about them. Integration has to
start at the *top* to take hold in this country, not in slums
where whites are scared blacks will take their jobs. The
visible role model of the upper classes must be the *first* to
demonstrate integration. But social workers in the South
Bronx try to integrate Italians, blacks, and Irish. When they
succeed, the family traditions and the economy fall apart,
leaving these people dependent on the state. In the old
days, a slum Italian could find a family connection; when
this ends, he winds up on welfare. This enforced self-
sustenance from above puts tremendous power in the hands
of the bureaucratic establishment.

Delancey's way to integrate is to start at the top, not because it's sweet or nice to be integrated, but because we've
been deluded so long about other people that we have to
surround ourselves with folks from all walks of life—and
then *stretch* to relate to them. This is opposed to what con-
ventionally passes as therapy, where upper-middle class
people who already agree on premises, sit around and
"identify" each other into a cheap "peak experience." Here,
we take people who can't relate, put them in a reality situation where they must learn to, and they come out stronger.
This applies to rich people as well as the slum addict. So we

move into the best neighborhoods and tell our leading citizens, "Look, you people *created* this problem, so we've dumped it right in your own back yard where you can't sweep it under the carpet. And now, by God, you better learn to *do* something about it!"

On New Year's Day 1971, Maher moved his entourage of twenty-five interracial ex-addicts into a commanding, three-story brick mansion in the heart of Pacific Heights, San Francisco's ultrafashionable and rigidly zoned residential area. Its twenty-nine rooms, plus nine separate baths, had once housed the consular corps of the United Arab Republic; it had stood empty since the Six-Day Arab-Israeli War of 1967, when Nasser announced that the Americans had bombed Egypt, because he didn't believe the Israelis capable of such a massive air strike. Thinking an Egypt-U.S.A. war was imminent, the Arabs vacated the building and left it in the hands of Coldwell-Banker, the largest real estate firm in the West, to sublet. During its three years of vacancy, the mansion had been repeatedly broken into and vandalized, making it even less enticing to prospective tenants, especially in Pacific Heights where zoning laws restricted its occupancy to a family of five.

Delancey Street set up headquarters in "Arabia" with the help of nearly a dozen lawyers, tax specialists, developers, and real-estate brokers—all former Synanon Game players who had transferred their loyalty to Maher's new group. One of them spotted the "For Lease" sign in the window and began negotiations with Coldwell-Banker in June 1970 for the move into the mansion for $1,000 a month rent. Maher went back to his interest-free loan sharks to borrow $2,000 for the first and last months' rent, gave the check to Coldwell-Banker, and signed a standard lease that was forwarded to the Arabs for their signature. Delancey Street's residents then began to clean up three years of vandalism and debris.

The pattern of harrassment encountered by Synanon

*when they moved into fancy neighborhoods was now re-
peated. A group of twenty-six neighbors sent a telegram to
the Arab's Special-Interest Section of the Indian Embassy in
Washington, warning that their San Francisco home had
been invaded by drug addicts, convicts, and whores. The
Arabs hired one of San Francisco's most prestigious law firms
to get them out.*

*One morning at 6:00, the police forcibly entered De-
lancey's plush new home with drawn pistols.*

JOHN MAHER: My night watchman was asleep on the
couch, and your basic Policeman O'Hara shoves a gun in his
face and barks, "Where's yer lease?" Now my night watchman is a Puerto Rican from Spanish Harlem where they
never heard of leases—you either pay the rent, or get out.
So he wakes up and says, "Lease? Officer, I ain't even got
no fuckin' *dog!*"

*Delancey's attorney Henry Hill countered with a visit to
the local station house, threatening the Police Department
with a lawsuit. He pressed into service Myron Moskowitz, a
Berkeley specialist in landlord-tenant law with experience on
behalf of tenants evicted on three days' notice. They filed
an action for declaratory release against the United Arab Republic, insuring that it would take at least two years to bring
the eviction case to court. Henry Hill discovered that under
the Foreign Agents Registration Act—a panicky holdover
from the Joe McCarthy era—the blue-chip law firm hired by
the Arabs was required to register with the government as the
agent of a foreign power. Since the firm had failed to comply
with this half-forgotten statute, Maher had lawyer Hill write
letters to the late J. Edgar Hoover and then Attorney General
John Mitchell, demanding that the law firm be indicted for
high treason.*

*The Arabs sent a polished diplomat from Washington
to negotiate. Hill hold him, "You've got everything to gain
and nothing to lose by leasing the building to us. We've*

spent hundreds of dollars cleaning the place, improving the property, preventing further vandalism, and we'll give the house back to you when the United Arab Republic re-establishes diplomatic relations with the U.S." Impressed by the immaculate transformation of a former disaster area, the Arab diplomat tabled all attempts to oust Maher for two years, only to resume hostilities when Nixon established relations with the new Egyptian leader Anwar Sadat.

After a long and heated zoning battle involving City Hall, a polarized Board of Supervisors, and front-page headlines, Delancey turned the empty, but spotless embassy back to the Sadat regime.

This did not mean that Delancey's people were homeless. They had leased seven other properties, and with an audacity that goaded the zoning authorities and the Pacific Heights Improvement Association to launch a redoubled attack, Maher purchased for $160,000 the sumptuous former home of the Soviet embassy, three blocks away from the Arabian mansion.

The purchase of what Delancey Streeters now called "Russia" was arranged by a cabal of former Synanon squares. Rubin Glickman, a young attorney who dabbled in restaurant management, was a specialist in real-estate law. Richard Kirschman spent six years developing San Francisco's Fox Plaza, a $23 million, thirty-three-story complex of apartments, business offices, and high-toned shops. They first met in an explosive Synanon Game and loathed each other on sight. After weeks of trading obscenities and indictments in Games, Glickman and Kirschman formed a close bond, born of their mutual boredom with routine money making, a need for social involvement, and their delight with Maher as Game player and companion. With Stanley Berney, a top realtor-developer they met in Games, they spearheaded the growth of Synanon's real-estate holdings. Glickman helped Dederich negotiate the purchase of Oakland's Athens Club for $750,000.

RUBIN GLICKMAN: Synanon developed their own in-house legal department, and no longer needed my services. When John Maher, whom I knew intimately in Games, started Delancey Street, he consulted me about real estate and legal problems. I was attracted to John's concept of putting the rehabilitated addict back in society, and besides, he needed my help, and Synanon didn't.

When forty-year-old Richard Kirschman dropped out of Synanon he went into semiretirement. The straight business world couldn't fill his emotional needs. He toured Europe, spent ten months working for Bernard Cornfeld's $30 million real-estate project in Spain. Returning to San Francisco, he dropped in to see what Maher was up to, and became a full-time director of Delancey Street.

RICHARD KIRSCHMAN: When it was clear that Delancey was outgrowing its Arabian home, we began eyeing the stately Russian mansion, originally for sale at $240,000. To-day, you couldn't build it for under half a million; no one would try. Do you know what it means—sixteen thousand square feet of a *single* family home in a rigidly zoned area? Who could buy it and keep it up in the 1970s? So the realtor kept reducing the price until Delancey bought it for $160,000. The Soviet Union occupied it only during the thirties and part of World War II, and after that it was empty. These neighborhood improvement fanatics who fear that Delancey Street destroys property values by moving into Pacific Heights are really comical; if we hadn't bought it, who knows how low the price would have dropped? Realtor Stanley Berney arranged Russia's first mortgage loan of $125,000 with a major savings and loan company that had done business with him for ten years. Now that's a lot of money for most people, but not for a major loan company when it comes to buying a prime piece of real estate worth twice that, in the classiest part of town.

RUBIN GLICKMAN: When a real-estate loan is made, the lender is more concerned with the value of the property than with who occupies it. Under the law, if the owner defaults on the loan, the company takes the property back, rather than sue for the defaulted payment, just like a loan company will repossess cars, instead of suing the owner for the unpaid balance. So when Delancey Street put $125,000 down for Russia, if the loan company forecloses they've bought a building worth a quarter of a million for $125,000 —very good business. It's also good business for Maher. What could he buy in a slum for $125,000? Our reasoning is, these rich mansions are no longer in vogue, they're in rigidly zoned areas, and no single family can afford to keep them up in these times.

The unpaid balance of $35,000 for Russia was raised by anonymous donors. This is all tax deductible, donated by presidents of large corporations, people in the public eye who often don't want their private affairs known. They are beholden to their stockholders and don't want their charitable donations to affect their public business interests. These are socially concerned people, mainly Jewish, very high up in business, society, and money circles.

Delancey's Finance Committee was headed by Janet Weinstein, widow of Rabbi Jacob Weinstein; their son Daniel is one of Delancey's aggressive young attorneys and Game players. Ms. Weinstein raised nearly $500,000 from San Francisco's Jewish community. One business patriarch in his eighties gave Maher $200,000 in cash to buy a complex of apartments in Marin County to house his growing band of residents.

An even more dramatic real-estate plunge than Russia was the debut of the Delancey Street Restaurant—complete with beer and wine license—in May 1973 in San Francisco's chic

Union Street shopping area. Richard Kirschman arranged to
purchase the business on a five-year lease, with an additional
five-year option, from Malcolm Stroud, proprietor of an eatery
with a hard-liquor license, the third business in a row to go
broke at this location. Stroud was asking $150,000 for the
long-closed restaurant; Kirschman negotiated to buy it for
$48,000 with $2,000 down, the balance to be paid, with no
interest, out of 5 percent of the gross receipts.

RICHARD KIRSCHMAN: Delancey sends Stroud a nickle
out of every dollar the restaurant grosses until the balance
is paid. In no way did our being a desirable social movement
influence Stroud to sell—it was purely a dollars and cents
proposition. By now, we had an excellent track record, financially. But mainly, Stroud could see this was a prime deal
because Delancey pays no salaries, which is always the biggest overhead for any restaurant. Also, people are intimidated
by the word *foundation,* which conjures up images of Rocke-
feller and Ford.

There never was any question about Delancey's ability to
meet its payments, based on our rate of growth, our work
and industries program, the fanatical dedication of our people, and our sources of private donors.

At one time our bank balance was up to $100,000—simple
arithmetic: In the Arabian mansion we had a hundred people
living, all of them working, and pooling their income. The
mansion rented for $1,000 a month, so these one hundred
tenants were paying $10 a month rent each. And since the
canned goods, meat, clothes, kitchen and office equipment
were all donated, the cash flow built up—and no one gets
paid a salary, not even John. Like everyone else who's been in
Delancey over eighteen months, he draws $20 a month walk-
ing-around money, or maybe a bit more when he needs it,
but he doesn't need much.

The Delancey Street Restaurant's intention to serve beer
and wine kicked off another hot controversy. For seven years,

hard liquor had been served at this location, but the Alcoholic Beverage Commission (A.B.C.) withheld a beer-and-
wine permit because Mon Singh Sandhu, the Foundations's
vice-president, spent five months in jail in 1970 for auto
theft and resisting arrest. The A.B.C. had agreed to grant the
license on condition that Delancey Street would not list a
felon as a corporate officer. Maher refused, "so that the pre-
cedent could be applied to all ex-convicts in California who
want to own and operate a small beer and liquor store."
Mike Berger, one of Delancey's attorneys, summoned a
platoon of respectable witnesses to testify at the A.B.C. hearings that Mon Sandhu had become a responsible citizen.
After a six-month struggle, the A.B.C. finally gave the restaurant the go-ahead to serve beer and wine.

RICHARD KIRSCHMAN: What was so unusual about this
move was the absolute trust John put in his people. I could
not imagine Synanon allowing their former addicts and alcoholics to work in a place where they had daily access to beer
and wine.

Maher made the new restaurant into "a mental flytrap
for bright, curious people." He hustled attractive tables and
chairs, up-to-date kitchen gear, and coaxed a top interior
decorator to design the establishment in keeping with the
posh boutiques, antique stores, and mod clothing shops in
the vicinity. Few would suspect that the smartly appointed
dinery, with its lush hanging ferns, gleaming copperware, and
uniformed waiters serving Crab Louis, French bread, and
Chablis, was operated and staffed solely by ex-convicts. The
restaurant became an in spot to dine, with Maher hosting
lunches for Karl Menninger, Cesar Chavez, and a fashion
show with gratis food and wine for the socialite volunteer
workers of the San Francisco International Film Festival, a
ploy that got the restaurant prime coverage on the society
pages of the major dailies.

The restaurant was only one of many sources of income

and outlets for putting Delancey's people to work in a chain of businesses that gross $80,000 a month. Maher opened an auto repair and body paint shop, leasing a cavernous garage for $1,400 a month to train mechanics and service a growing fleet of cars, buses, and moving vans pooled by residents and donated by friends. Reconstructing vintage Rolls Royces and Bentleys became a specialty. Stan Berney found an antique London double-decker bus wasting away in a Los Angeles junk yard. The auto shop put this relic in running order, resplendent in red with gold trim, to transport residents, while Maher dreamed up future schemes to combine his penchant for socially pointed put-ons with his constant scrounging for funds.

JOHN MAHER: This double-decker will be used as a parody of the guided tour. White people will have to sit in the rear. For $5.00 we'll take tourists, not to the Top of the Mark or Fisherman's Wharf, but to the ghettos, the jail, Juvenile Hall, the tenderloin, and the tour will end outside Mayor Alioto's home where the tourists will give him their reaction to what they've seen. We'll charge the criminology and sociology departments of local universities to use our Reality Tour as an adjunct to classroom instruction.

A potted plant and door-to-door terrarium business was born in the spacious greenhouse atop the Russian mansion. Redwood burl tables were manufactured in the basement. At Christmas 1974, Delancey branched out to sell holiday trees, yule logs, and poinsettias in vacant lots provided by sympathetic realtors.

Plumbing, roofing, and construction are done on a cash or barter basis. In return for painting the Drew School, a private academy with rigid scholastic standards, Delancey enrolled a group of teen-age residents on scholarships. An advertising specialties sales force, headed by Mary Nutter, a former WAC captain in World War II, sells imprinted ball-point pens, lighters, and office supplies to firms throughout California, Washington, and Oregon. Friends in the cinema trades keep tabs on what movies are shot in San Francisco, whose roller-coaster streets are catnip to prominent film makers. When the directors of Airport, The Candidate, and What's Up, Doc? were looking for convict types and extras, they hired these spear carriers from Delancey Street.

Some of the city's most extensive property owners hire Delancey people to run their rental and complaint offices, paint, fix plumbing. Willie Brown, the dapper black California Assemblyman, employs residents to repair his house.

WILLIE BROWN: If John Maher was in an illegitimate business he'd be the king of racketeers. I never in my life ran into anyone with this much know-how about bartering, trading, and hustling free goods and services.

To store the daily flow of donated vehicles, clothes, books, household appliances, and furniture, Maher leased the vacant half-mile long Pier 41 on San Francisco's Embarcadero for $1 a month.

For a $250 fee, Delancey Street conducts a Crime School Clinic for Bay Area store managers and security officers, with demonstrations on how to spot rip-off artists, shoplifters, and pickpockets. Jane Rudovich shows how she stole thousands of dollars from four leading department stores that employed her as sales clerk—without once being caught. Alice Smith, who perfected shoplifting skills to support her drug habit, tells how contacts working within a store tipped her off to loose security measures. Morris Hodges faked noisy heart attacks to distract clerks while his cronies emptied the cash registers. Tom Grapshi, who made the "most wanted" list of the New York Fifth Avenue Merchants Association, tells how racial prejudice is a common tool used by shoplifters: "I'd tell a clerk to watch some black who was acting suspicious, and while they were alerted, I'd just beat them blind."

Residents and friends are put to work selling $1 tickets

to the annual raffle, which grossed $86,000 in 1974; as third prize, Delancey Street "promises not to move into your neighborhood for one year."

When Maher talked the New Yorker, Newsweek, and New York magazine into running a series of free full-page ads, they advised him to hire a professional ad agency to do the layout, but "being in the business of self-reliance, we do all the ads ourself." Dugald Sturmer, the former art director of Ramparts magazine and a Delancey square, designs and pastes up all ads, posters, flyers, and the Foundation's house organ, Rap Sheet. Ed Turnbull, Maher's parochial school buddy, is the staff photographer.

The most ambitious venture into printed propaganda is the Delancey Street Journal, a flagrant stylistic copy of the Wall Street Journal that includes a twelve-page supplement of editorial opinions by local writers, civic leaders, union officials, and consumer advocates who can sound off on any subject—as long as it has nothing to do with Delancey Street. Editor Pat Donnelly, who came out of San Quentin after a six-year stretch for burglary, supervised the distribution of six hundred thousand free copies. As usual, everything connected with the Delancey Street Journal, the printing, the paper, was donated.

Each evening, Delancey's trucks make the rounds of three bakeries that contribute day-old doughnuts and bread. Maher sends his paisanos to the wholesale produce area to hustle: "Hey, Nunzio! Leave us have some of them bruised tomatoes, you gonna throw them out anyway."

The California National Park Service provides an unusual source of income. Five days a week Delancey takes fifty slum children (the group changes weekly) to Alcatraz Island, site of the abandoned federal prison, where five Delancey residents relate their experiences in jail and on heroin. Following their firsthand shock therapy, the kids go to a cook-out at Fort Baker's white-hand Pacific beach. "The youngsters," says

Maher, "are smart enough to perceive the difference between the two areas of water sport." The Park Service pays Delancey $10,000 for this ten-week project.

Although Maher will not accept federal grants, five neighboring counties contribute $100 a month for each of the three dozen addicts sent to Delancey on probation; this program is headed by John's youngest brother Billy.

BILLY MAHER: There are absolutely no strings attached to these county subsidies, and since it costs over $175 a month to feed, house, and clothe one of our residents, the counties are more than getting their money's worth.

As the Foundation got nationwide publicity, more judges and parole officers sent addicts to Delancey Street rather than to jail. Murray Greenfield, for seven years a sergeant of the San Quentin guards, and currently assistant supervisor of San Francisco's Parole Board, placed five parolees with Maher.

MURRAY GREENFIELD: It worked beyond my expectations. I remember our first meeting in Delancey, me, my supervisor, and ten parolees. Now, we're a pretty hardened bunch, but Maher charmed the hell out of all of us. All the people we sent there stayed. We know they're okay because we've got great confidence in the place. My feelings about Delancey are mixed, because basically it's against what I always *thought* I believed. It's highly disciplined, highly directed, and you know there's always one man in charge.

I remember one time I was there when three men who had split came back and asked to be accepted again. Maher gave them a chewing out right in the hall where everyone could hear. Now, I was a sergeant at San Quentin for nearly eight years, and you know something? I couldn't *take* it! I thought I'd heard everything, but this was just too terrible to believe—and yet it works. The place doesn't make you feel depressed like most of these government-funded halfway houses. In some of those outfits, dope dealers can not only hustle outside the door, but even inside the premises. I can't see any other workable alternative for former addicts and prisoners. Delancey Street provides these people with a reason to live, and this the establishment hasn't been able to do.

Besides a reason to live, Delancey's people needed room to live. They were sleeping on pool tables and in hallways in both the Arabian and Russian houses. In December 1973, Maher again startled the community, making headlines with the purchase of two prime pieces of property to house his three hundred residents.

The Ebbtide, a thirty-six-unit apartment with swimming pool and a commanding bayside view of Sausalito, connected to San Francisco by the Golden Gate Bridge, was purchased for $649,500 of which $188,000 was in cash:

JOHN MAHER: Built in the mid-fifties, the Ebbtide apartments are typical West Los Angeles-style garbage, so we put our people to work refurbishing the structure to fit more into the character of the community.

At the same time, Rubin Glickman arranged the purchase of El Portel, a five-story apartment and restaurant adjoining Golden Gate Park, two blocks from its complex of art museum, planetarium, aquarium, and famed Japanese Tea Garden.

JOHN MAHER: We had our eye on a dozen other properties and decided El Portel is the one in which we will be cheated least. The building was purchased at the exorbitant price of $776,000—it cost all our treasury. Not one cent was donated by Delancey Street's zoning opposition, who had been so loud in proclaiming their desire to help us move out of Pacific Heights.

CHAPTER SIX

A Community
Divided

*"Descendants of horse thieves with the pretentions
of the Hapsburgs."*

JOHN MAHER: When we bought the El Portel
and Ebbtide apartments, this attracted endless numbers of
inspectors, enough to build the Aswan Dam, and all at taxpayers' expense. El Portel had stood there half a century, and
suddenly these petty functionaries discover certain problems.
Because we cure drug addicts, they decide we're running a
hospital in a non-hospital zone.

In Mill Valley, permits that were obviously legal were
turned down, so we're forced to piss away our time and energies in lawsuits. The owner of a long-empty supermarket,
vandalized over the years by the drug-crazed upper-class children of Marin County, let us have it rent free in return for
painting and fixing it up. Once we put this supermarket in
perfect order, the authorities came around and told us this
wasn't a conforming use. Meanwhile our maintenance crew,
rushing to get the thirty-six unit Ebbtide so it was fit to live
in, is constantly stopped by the police: "Who are you?
Where are you going? Where's your permit?"

The bureaucracy has become so big that old-fashioned conspiracy is no longer necessary, like in the Winning of the West, when a bunch of guys sit around a table saying, "Foreclose all the mortgages, get the populace out of Kansas, and then we can run through the railroad." What happens today is, the little fish in the bureaucracy get the hint from the big guys and then act on cue: "Isn't it a shame that Maher is permitted to abuse the citizenry and openly flout the law?" Translated, this means, "*Get* the motherfucker." Once City Hall called its dogs out on us, it was impossible to call them back because that would imply collusion with that small group of the socially retarded rich who were trying to drive us out of their Pacific Heights neighborhood, recent descendants of horse thieves and robber barons who have pretentions to being San Francisco's equivalent of the Hapsburgs.

Leader of the fight to oust Delancey Street from the Arabian and Russian mansions is Peter Fay, owner of a men's haberdashery, a neighbor of Maher's, and president of the Pacific Heights Improvement Association. Fay alerted the City Planning Commission to Delancey's infraction of the zoning ordinance limiting residence to "either a family in the traditional sense, or a maximum of five unrelated individuals."

PETER FAY: My group supports the purpose of Delancey Street, but to be honest, prefer them *not* to be in our neighborhood, especially when they are in naked violation of our zoning laws. In the 1972 election, some twenty-seven people were living there, registered for McGovern. On the other hand, as long as the Arab and Soviet consulates are being occupied, we prefer they do as Maher has done, by adhering to the laws, keeping the place up—they've even made extensive improvements—and causing no trouble. But we're taxed to death here, and some of our members feel the value of their property may be lowered by having a halfway house move in. Also, these Delancey people have their cars parked all over, what with their constant symposiums and streams of visitors, so that neighbors can't park in front of their own homes. Still, we prefer these people to having the places stand empty with the attendant vandalism. And I must admit that I haven't talked to a person in Delancey Street that I haven't liked—particularly John Maher. It would be very hard to work up a dislike for him on a personal basis.

When I went to Delancey Street for my first and only visit, Maher greeted me with a big friendly handshake and said, "Well, I think we're going to get along great—we're both from Ireland!" Frankly, it was a most pleasant talk. He told me the aims of his organization and asked my opinion. I told him it was illegal occupancy of the Arab consulate. They had no lease at the time, and it was occupied without the consent of the owners.

JOHN MAHER: I did an extreme right-wing John Birch number on him: "Mr. Fay, are you going to take the side of the Arabs, oil blackmailers who would deny our country its lifeblood? Allies of the *Russians?* Are you actually going to take the part of a Communist power against American citizens? Do you support creeping socialism by forcing our people back to the slums, on welfare, at taxpayers' expense, instead of having them work at honest jobs, like they do here? Now, I don't know if you're just a dupe, or if you're an out-and-out Communist, but . . ." We hung the biggest American flag we could find outside, and the guy was utterly smashed.

"George Spelvin," a wealthy socialite who asks to remain anonymous, was upset when Delancey moved into Russia, a few blocks away from his showplace home.

GEORGE SPELVIN: Of course I'm worried about my property values. I spent a great deal of money buying this house in an expensive area that is now overrun with undesirables. Two Delancey people, obviously drunk as skunks, tore up two large potted plants outside my house. No, I didn't call Delancey Street about it, but I knew where they were from because their heads were shaved. I have it on good authority that when they moved out of the Arab consulate, they left the place an ungodly mess. No, I didn't stop in to look, but this is what I heard. And I'd like to know just how many addicts are really cured at this place, and how many people split? What's the *percentage?* They never tell you that."

JOHN MAHER: This is the cliché response of those who deliberately choose not to understand what we're doing. Somehow, I just can't imagine anyone walking up to Captain John Smith and asking him how many Pilgrims split and went back to England that first year at Plymouth Rock. The Pilgrims were on hostile terrain, trying to build a society that would last. Some froze to death, some were killed by Indians. Those who endured went on to found a culture that produced Hawthorne, Emerson, Thoreau, Margaret Fuller, Melville, and Whitman.

But the bureaucratic mind loves to recite figures of splitees, whether these figures mean anything or not. We could cure all the addicts in America if we blinded them and left them in the Mojave Dessert. This would be considered a cure by the government, which wouldn't notice it cost us millions in Medicare, destroyed the lives of the addicts, and polluted the desert. These people who pick us apart by saying, "What about the ones you *don't* cure?" are the same ones who asked, "What happened to all those poor blacks in Alabama *after* Martin Luther King left their community? I don't know how much good he really did them . . ." And the establishment has got this bullshit down to an art form. They'd much rather talk about the ones we *can't* help, rather than the ones we can.

A local columnist of what used to be called the smart set spotted Maher at a fashionable society function and, in pursuit of material, asked him why he came to cocktail parties? "To find someone I can use—I'm ruthless." This reply, with a three-column photo of its maker, formed the head of her next Chronicle column, reinforcing the fears of Neighborhood Improvementers that Maher meant to take over, and not just in Pacific Heights.

Maher took care to ingratiate himself with the more liberal element in the neighborhood. When Georgina Callan, a fixture in San Francisco's Social Register, moved into her new home two doors away from Arabia, her doorbell rang and "two terribly attractive kids were there with pots of flowers. They said, 'We're the Delancey Street welcoming committee, and if there's anything you need, just let us know.' A few months later my house was broken into, and I went to Delancey Street for help."

JOHN MAHER: I assigned two of my roughest looking ex-burglars to walk patrol. It takes one to know one. Our guys saw some obvious hood on the street and told him, "Look, we don't believe in violence, but you are in a violent business, and violence begets violence, so if you show your ass in this neighborhood again, we're gonna break your fuckin' legs."

Arabia's next-door neighbors, Indonesian Consul General John Sedunk and his wife Felicia, admitted some dismay when Delancey moved in.

FELICIA SEDUNK: But they arrived with flowers and invited me next door. My first visit dispelled all fears. There had been talk at fashionable luncheons with society women asking, "Do you really feel safe living next door to all those rough people?" And I tell them I have not encountered neighbors more friendly. The youngest of my three children, my sixteen year old, is over there most of the time, drying dishes, and I ask him, "Why don't you dry the dishes at *my* house?" His English is greatly improved, if somewhat colorful. My husband tends to be supportive, since he spent ten months in jail for revolutionary acts against the Dutch in Indonesia during the forties.

John Maher.

The Delancey Street maintenance garage on Sacramento
Street. Restoring vintage Bentleys and Rolls Royces is a spe-
ciality of the garage.

The Delancey Street Restaurant in San Francisco's Union Street shopping area.
Left, the double-decker bus outside Delancey's El Portel apartments ("Egypt") with a load of day-camp children on their way to Alcatraz to inspect the "dog kennels" that once housed federal prisoners.

"Arabia"—former consulate of the United Arab Republic
in San Francisco's exclusive Pacific Heights—the first
Delancey Street mansion.

John Maher (right) locking horns with Quentin Kopp,
member of San Francisco's Board of Supervisors and leader of the
City Hall faction to oust Delancey Street from Pacific Heights.

MICHELLE VIGNES

John Maher and
Dr. Mimi Silbert.

Dr. Mimi Silbert.

ED TURNBULL

ED TURNBULL

ON FACING PAGE
A Delancey Street wedding.

John Maher with Randolph A. Hearst who enlisted Delancey Street's help in distributing the $2 million "Food Giveaway" following the alleged kidnapping of his daughter Patty Hearst.

John Maher talks to two staff members in Delancey's "Russian" mansion.

MICHELLE VIGNES

John Maher addresses Cesar Chavez's Farmworkers Union during the strikers' march to Modesto, California.

JOHN MAHER: Consul Sedunk asked me to put his son to work on our construction crew, because he's afraid the kid will grow up effete from running around foreign schools with nothing but rich, weak sons of ambassadors.

When another neighbor Myra Frankel, donated five thousand pieces of art to the annual auction to raise funds for KQED-TV, the local Public Broadcasting outlet, Delancey Street volunteered to truck this considerable load to the auction.

Aside from the die-hard opposition led by Peter Fay, Maher had wired himself into his new community by the time the move to oust him from Pacific Heights took a serious turn. When the city's eviction order was upheld by the Board of Permit Appeals, sixty rich and socially prominent neighbors signed a petition in protest, many of them testifying in Maher's behalf during the months-long hearings that packed the Board of Supervisors palatial chambers. These hot-tempered proceedings attracted stockbrokers, coiffeured saloniers, Cesar Chavez's Farm Workers, waving red and black "Viva La Huelga" banners, the Prisoners' Union, senior citizens, and gay liberation. Maher had given active support to all these groups, helping the Farm Workers picket, busing the aged to the polls, and getting sixty-four-year-old Wesley Robert Wells out of prison after forty-six years.

Maher cemented strong ties to top politicians in the Bay Area, helping to get out the vote for Congressman John Burton, and supporting his brother Philip, San Francisco's prime-moving congressman, who was elected to the powerful post of Chairman of the Democratic Caucus in the House revolt after the 1974 elections. Two of Delancey's most vocal champions on the Board of Supervisors are its former Chairwoman, Dianne Feinstein, and George Moscone, the front runner in San Francisco's 1975 mayoralty race.

WILLIE BROWN: Maher has built such a firm political base, and made so many friendships with people in authority, that *nobody* could move him out of Pacific Heights, and when the city tried, I was glad to be of some help.

Unexpected support came from Randolph A. Hearst, publisher-heir of the newspaper empire, who declared himself indebted to Delancey Street for its role in salvaging his $2 million food giveaway demanded by the Symbionese Liberation Army (SLA) as a condition for the release of his apparently kidnapped daughter, Patricia. When the giveaway began in February 1974, one truck with food for four thousand poor was hijacked, theft at the food warehouse was rampant, and the entire program in a confessed state of shambles. A. Ludlow Kramer, director of People In Need (PIN), in charge of the giveaway, appealed to Maher for help. For seven days Delancey worked twelve-hour shifts, unloading produce at the dock, packaging goods, loading trucks, and riding shotgun to the distribution centers.

A. LUDLOW KRAMER: From the day Delancey Street's people were around, no one dared rip anything off. We lost nothing. They were absolutely tremendous, real heroes. They would accept none of the food, and wouldn't take a nickle for their services.

This caper got bigger play in the Los Angeles papers than in San Francisco, where the anti-Delancey forces had long since abandoned talk of undersirables and stuck to the charge that Maher was violating the zoning laws. They were joined by the Egyptian embassy in Washington that wanted their consulate returned now that diplomatic relations with the U.S. had been re-established. In the Board of Supervisor hearings that were making daily headlines, Maher claimed his people had no place to go and he was not moving them back to the slums. The Board passed a resolution "commending and supporting Delancey Street for outstanding service to the community" and creating an ad hoc Citizens' Committee, requesting the city attorney and others "to stay prosecution of complaint for eviction," urging the citizens to "assist in discovering an alternate location which will not infringe upon existing zoning laws and yet will provide an environment conducive to the Delancey Street program.

On August 8, 1974, amid an aura of good will between Delancey Street and the Egyptian consulate, which expressed its "warmest admiration for its tenants of the past three years and recommended them as tenants to any and all possible future landlords," Maher moved his entourage out of the Arabian mansion. Accompanied by a brass band with bagpipes, and dressed in army khakis, the smiling parade of former addicts marched briskly to a new home half a block away—the forty-room Estonia Residential Club that Delancey had purchased a month before for $250,000. With the Russian mansion just around the corner from Estonia, Delancey Street now had two permanent outposts in Pacific Heights, though the fight to oust them continues.

JOHN MAHER: Across the street from Russia are ensconsed a bunch of private detectives tailing us—we wave to them every morning. These shadows are hired by the Neighborhood Improvement nuts. My lawyers don't cost me anything, and theirs cost them a fortune. They will piss away their patrimony trying to get rid of me, and I will remain. All my people will remain, and when we die, our children will remain.

CHAPTER SEVEN

San Francisco's Magic Christian

"When you're incompetent, and got no education,
you can be either one of two things: you can be a bum,
or a great social leader. I failed as a bum,
so I had no options."

When San Quentin released Mike Killean after a six-year stretch for armed robbery, he made the front page with a little help from his friends.

Killean was met at the main gate by three glistening Cadillac limousines driven by chauffers in pearl-grey tunics with caps and puttees of black leather. Lounging with heavy-lidded insolence in the plush back seats were six Havana-puffing Godfathers in black fedoras, wrap-around sunglasses, $50 silk shirts, hand-painted ties, and double-breasted pinstripes.

The head Mafioso in the lead car flipped the switch that lowered the window, crooked his finger at the guard and growled, "Hey you—git our friend over here. Quick!"

"Yes-sir!" With hurried deference, the guard escorted Killean to the car where the Godfather kissed him on both cheeks, handed him a cigar, made room for him in the back seat, and signaled the caravan to drive slowly away.

Someone tipped off the newsmen that the Mob was pick-

ing up a buddy, and a four-column photo of this bizarre pro-
cession made page one of the San Francisco Chronicle, which
with little probing, learned that Killean's reception committee was not the Mafia, but the Delancey Street Foundation in rented limousines and borrowed pinstripes.

JOHN MAHER: The main purpose of this socially pointed
practical joke was, as usual, lost on the newspapers. We
wanted to dramatize how our idiotic prison system makes
the guards as much of a victim as the inmates. Suppose our
friend at San Quentin was met by a cruddy Ford pickup
driven by some slob in shitty dungarees. Know what the guard
would have said? "Git that truck away from the main gate,
take it around to the back, we'll let this asshole out when
we're fuckin' well ready—and what's that in yer coat?" So
what *we* do is drive up like crass hoodlums, but *rich* ones,
and the guards fell all over themselves; one even touched his
cap in a salute. They've been programmed to respond to a
symbol: "Anyone who drives a block-long Cad and dresses
that expensively must know somebody *important,* may know
the governor, the warden, someone who can cost me a pro-
motion if I'm not nice to him." We've got to find a way to
unite the working classes like these prison guards who have
this silly notion they're part of the establishment.

After the Godfather caper, Delancey Street's construction
crew built atop a flat-bed trailer an exact replica of a San
Quentin two-man cell—10 feet long, 4½ feet wide, 7 feet tall
—with two narrow stacked bunks, toilet, sink, and mirror. An
outside wall bore the warning, "This is not the answer!"
Maher towed the trailer to the marble steps of San Francisco's City Hall during its bustling lunch hour. Locked behind the bars of the mock-up cell were two of Delancey's
blue-denimed ex-cons, chatting with an uneasy crowd of
judges, district attorneys, and a rapt class of twelve-year-old
pupils touring City Hall for their civics lesson; they couldn't
believe the cell was so small.

"Don't you go crazy?"

"Of course. Nothing to do. You don't learn anything in here except how to commit different or better crimes."

"What kind of food do you get in there?"

"Terrible. Oatmeal mush in the morning with no sugar; watery pea soup and bologna sandwiches for lunch. How would you like thirteen years of bologna sandwiches?"

Maher selected his felons with care.

JOHN MAHER: One of our inmates was educated, articulate, but the other was someone even some nut bigot could identify with, lot of time in jail, punchy, no teeth left from fighting cops, because that's the way prison *is*, not some David Niven movie, but a *lumpenproletariate* milieu. You may find a few self-educated people, a hip embezzler or schoolteacher, but they're rare. You got to steal more than $100,000 *not* to go to jail. Chuck Colson got out after seven months, Mr. Agnew is playing golf, but Wesley Robert Wells has been in jail forty-six years for stealing two pairs of pants, and I can't get the marijuana initiativers and the peace-and-freedom lovers to demonstrate, organize the voters, block the San Quentin lines to get this man out. Wells was black before it was chic, and paid a terrible price for it. All these kids like Stokely and Cleaver come *after* him. His body's covered with knife wounds, he's in his sixties and dying. The establishment won't let him out because he's not enough of a pop-hero to make his release politically expedient, and the liberals won't support me and turn out for Wells because it's not *groovy* enough. [Wells was released from prison July 1, 1974, through the efforts of Delancey Street.]

Wells in 1932 killed a man in prison, not uncommon in California, where the murderers are generally the *sane* people. Fifty prisoners were stabbed this year in San Quentin. Why? The California Corrections budget is up for review in the state legislature. Now to dramatize how much more money they need, it was necessary for the prison authorities to start a *riot*, to upset the support-your-local-police tricks, and the police themselves. Immediately when the budget came up for review in Sacramento, the word came down from the Department of Corrections to the warden of San Quentin, "Integrate the Adjustment Center," where the blacks are guerrillas, the white's are Nazis, all locked in cages because they're alleged too dangerous to run loose among the other nuts. Now it's very interesting that they chose *this* moment to integrate that group, making sure that no guards were stationed in that area. Bloodshed *instantly* spread throughout the prison, so in Sacramento they were saying, "Unless we get another $5 million to control this situation, God knows what'll happen!" Two days after the riot, Sacramento voted the money.

I predicted Reagan would build these two new jails, and I don't think he'll close San Quentin like he's been saying. For four years they've been holding up paroles and giving longer sentences with one thought in mind—jam San Quentin, which has grown from fourteen hundred to twenty-five hundred, create riots, and then go to the poor taxpayer and say, "The only way to control these riots is to build more prisons," which will be given out for patronage. Fascinating that the California legislature turned both these new prisons down, and now they're back in an election year. Both proposed new prisons are in rural areas where unemployment is high; one in Southern California near the Mexican border to give them a share of the patronage, and the other in Solano County to lock in the farm vote because the dairies are going under. Now, all this has nothing to do with prisoners! It has to do with the economics of the state and patronage. And if these new prisons don't go through, Reagan will tell us, "We tried, only to be subverted by the forces of Communism and terror."

In California, where people are worried about mental health, the government builds mental hospitals. Any *sane* person could have told them in front, that what they were building wouldn't work, so they build them to create giant patronage. Then, when the bureaucrats need the taxpayers' vote, they say, "Do away with mental hospitals and save money," so the taxpayers are happy Reagan is cutting the budget. Then they turn around and say, "We have to lock in the unemployment-conscious vote," so they build two new prisons! Endless, crazy round-robin! We have eighteen mental institutions in California, and a number of them are closing, so why do we have to build new prisons? If we *must* have this insane prison system, why don't we just use the mental hospitals and build *walls* around them?

Reagan's political position is unassailable. Since the mental hospitals don't work, and in fact torture people, he neutralizes the left-liberals by closing them, and pacifies right-wing taxpayers who are "tired of carrying these indigents on our rolls." They didn't see the relationship between closing mental hospitals, cutting off psychiatric care, and the increase of rape and murder in the streets, anymore than these taxpayers saw the relationship between bombing Indo-China, and their children, who didn't want to go get shot, going a little crazy.

We built this mock-up cell and tow it all over town because we want these taxpayers to witness the incredible insanity of putting a youngster in one of these cages with Nazi hoodlums, motorcycle riders running in gangs, assaultive homosexual rapists, Mexicans who think they're the Mafia, some kill-the-honkie black guerrillas, and twenty Charlie Manson types. What happens is that any *sane* man kills anybody who gets too close to him, not because he's a bad guy, but because he'd have to be crazy to do anything else. Ten years later they unloose this snarling animal, fighting to survive, on society and his family. You lock a dog in a cage, terrorize and abuse it every day, and when you open the cage two years later, the dog doesn't lick your hand for letting it out—the dog takes a healthy bite out of your ass.

While Maher passed out protest postcards to Governor Reagan, a furious woman was shaking under his nose the morning's headline of a cop-killer in Oakland: "Why don't you do-gooder, bleeding-hearts show a little sympathy for the widow of this policeman, the victims of these monsters you protect and coddle?" and flounced off before Maher could answer.

JOHN MAHER: What this poor woman doesn't realize is that these kinds of horrendous crimes are such a small minority. Most people in jail are there for smoking pot, bad checks, boosting a car. Obviously the whacko in Chicago who killed nine nurses belongs in a hospital, but what about the nineteen-year-old purple heart veteran who got hooked in Vietnam, came back, hung out with the wrong crowd, and got ten years in the slammer? People have to be unsold on this idiot notion of *punishment*. Arguments against prison reform are arguments against the taxpayers' own interests. You drive men crazy by locking them in cages like this one and, in or out, they cost you *money*. We've got to teach middle-class people about prison reform. The radicals and honest conservatives dig the issues, just like sane liberals do, because they're intense people. It's this large vacuous mass of the uncommitted middle that's still hung up on the fantasy of *punishing* people. But that poor woman was right when she said we "coddle criminals"—Nixon, Agnew, the head of General Motors that turns out unsafe cars, but what we *don't* coddle are poor people, blacks, Chicanos, or ghetto prostitutes.

Maher pulled his next front-page stunt on Valentine's Day 1972. His crew hustled some slightly stale chocolates from a friendly five-and-dime manager, collected crushed flowers from the wholesale produce market, and sprung with

Delancey's last money for a hundred cartons of cigarettes. In an unprecedented move, San Francisco's reform Sheriff Richard Hongisto let Delancey Street into the women's jail where they gifted the astonished prisoners with flowers, candy, and smokes. "It was wonderful bedlam," said the Sheriff, "No one believed it. One prisoner said it was the nicest thing that happened to her in sixty years."

JOHN MAHER: "Here's where you need prison reform. These bureaucrats keep thinking if they change the paint from beige to green, or put more salt in the lima beans, things'll get better; they won't. What *will* help is the recognition that these prisoners are human beings.

The godfather caper at San Quentin, the mock prison cell at City Hall, and the St. Valentine's Day party at the women's jail were the first in a series of Magic Christian pranks pulled by Maher to get the attention of a community he was to polarize from the mayor's office to the ghetto.

CHAPTER EIGHT

Mimi

"I'm determined to purge the macho *hangover
from the street."*

After Mimi Silbert met John Maher at Christ-
mas 1972, she brought great changes to Delancey Street and
its founder, who declared himself in love for the first time in
his thirty-two years.

JOHN MAHER: When you live the way I do, you can't
get involved with women who still have the conventional
slave mentality, always whining that you never take them to
the movies when the 16th Assembly District is in flames.
Mimi's a grown woman who says, "Great—you do your
thing and I'll do mine, and help you do yours."

My past relations with women were consistent with my
rotten attitude toward people in general. My first exposure
to sex at age eleven was your basic gang-bang situation. A
Spanish whore, stoned out of her mind, decided to throw a
freebie to one of the kids in the neighborhood bar. (In those
days you could stand at the bar when you were six or seven,
and they'd give you a beer because they thought it was
cute.) This was my initiation into a series of gang-bangs with
retarded teen-age girls or local whores, most of whom ended
up dead of an overdose, or in the nut house. In those days
before women's lib, we found in Catholic society there are

good girls and bad girls. Bad girls, it doesn't matter what happens to them, fuck 'em, they should all get cancer because they're useless except for a screw, while good girls should be frigid and cry a lot.

When I came to Synanon, Dederich and his wife Bettye cleaned up *some* of my thinking about women, urging us to honor the marriage contract, not lie to our mates.

Betty and I were living together in the Santa Monica house and got married in a shotgun wedding when Dederich didn't want trouble with local blue noses trying to close him down. What went wrong with our marriage was that I was cheating on her. As long as I was going to lie to her and live by the Playboy philosophy, we couldn't have a workable marriage. She found out I was cheating because I told her in a Game. Outwardly she took it calmly, but after the Game she went on a Citizen Kane rampage, slashing my clothes and busting the furniture—couldn't handle it. I didn't chippie around all that much, but once you cheat on a person, you cut off all lines of communication with them. I acted like a spoiled child. I didn't get into the philosophy of sexual and emotional containment, so when a problem came up between Betty and me, instead of working it out with her, I ran around the block and picked up an airline stewardess. This always leads to disaster. I knew it was my fault, but I either had to spend two years rebuilding the marriage or chuck it; so I chucked it, knowing I had neglected my responsibility and not lived up to the nuptial agreement. I could rationalize it like these Playboy creeps, "Why not explore the freedom of our bodies?" But this doesn't work when you try to relate to a wife who doesn't think that way.

When Maher started Delancey Street, he was sleeping up front with a woman from the outside, careful to observe the taboo against sexual involvement between staff members and resident dope fiends.

JOHN MAHER: This was openly discussed in Games. I

was never emotionally involved with her and told her so
repeatedly. I treated her like a concubine. Love never came
into it at all. It never did, until I met Mimi.

A yin to Maher's yang, thirty-two-year-old Mimi Silbert
springs from Boston Jewish intellectuals with Old World
roots. Voted "most likely to" throughout high school and
college, at twenty-one she won first prize for an American
philosophical treatise and went to Paris to study under Jean-
Paul Sartre. After getting a double Ph.D in psychology and
criminology at Berkeley in 1968, she worked with Dr. Richard Korn, sociologist Lewis Yablonsky [author of Synanon:
The Tunnel Back] and became a protégé of Dr. Bernard
Diamond, famed West Coast psychiatric criminologist. Besides her growing involvement with Delancey Street on a
policy-making level, she continues her long-time function
as San Francisco State College's Director of Institutional
Change, a program urging students out of the classroom and
into the community. She acts as consultant to the Berkeley
Police Department, Letterman Hospital, the Alameda County
Delinquent Program, and the San Diego Police Department
where she trains officers to handle community relations. She
got a $1 million grant from The National Institute of Mental
Health (NIMH) to set up and administer encounter groups
in Berkeley.

Mimi belies the conventional clichés about social workers.
An arresting beauty, she has an aura of what used to be called
"an old-fashioned girl." She was not taken with Maher on
first meeting.

MIMI SILBERT: John's brother Billy invited me to Delancey for advice on how to apply for a grant. In the middle
of our talk, John walks over, coming on strong, very *macho*
with "Hi, sweetie!" and I was less than thrilled with this
routine. That night he phoned: "Listen—got to talk to you
right away about getting this grant," and I agreed to meet
him in Berkeley the next morning.

We sat in John's car to discuss the grant—and it was

instant magic between us, sitting there beaming at each other like a couple of idiots. Suddenly John yells, "To *hell* with the $1 million grant—let's go to the country!" We found ourselves sitting in a remote meadow, never touching, not even holding hands, but telling with our eyes. Suddenly, here I am, with a conventionally happy eight-year marriage to a man I adored, never slept with anyone but my husband, 5½-year-old twin boys, never a thought of divorce—what am I doing?

John drove me home from the country and my husband met me at the top of the stairs. He took one look at me and said, "Oh, *fuck!*" He could see it was all over my face. That night I told him the truth: "I don't know what's going to happen, you know I don't have whims or caprices, but I'm tremendously taken with this man and what he's doing. I know it sounds girlish and impulsive, but we both intuitively feel we were born for each other. I'm not planning to get sexually involved, but I do know that I'm going to have to spend a lot of time with him."

My husband is very quiet, but terribly strong. His response was that it would wear off, that John was overwhelmingly dynamic, but lacked holding power. In the end it wouldn't last.

Next day, John went into a funk, closed himself in his room for three days, and called a mutual friend, Richard Korn. "This is *it* for me! I have to be with this woman!" Dick Korn is a big, romantic slob and he told John, "Whisk her off her feet!" which infuriated him. "You crazy? A married woman, with two kids? What kind of romantic horseshit irresponsibility is that?"

Two days later, John and I found we felt the same way about each other. He asked me, "Would you be my mistress?"

"No!"

"Thank God you said that! We've got to do this thing *right!*"

He really scared hell out of me because he was so *sure*.
"Of *course* we have to get married, of *course* it has to work!"
This kind of commitment terrified me, and we both felt
tremendous guilt, which we talked over endlessly, with me
writing a three-act Jewish play about why it wouldn't work,
and John telling me what an asshole he was, going through
these numbers like, "Women *do* things like this when they're
thirty, after eight years of marriage—is that it?"

We saw each other constantly, growing unbelieveably
close. Since we never went to bed, we restaurant-hopped,
five meals a day, putting on weight, and John was so open
about everything, so tender, not *macho* at all.

Two months after I met John, I separated from my husband, feeling I had more energy going out toward John
and knowing it was unfair. I was always dogged by this
overpowering sense of guilt. My husband was hurt, angry,
but he's a marvelous person who said, "You take your
chances. I can't say I'll be here if you come back, and I
can't say I won't."

For the next six months, John and I were inseparable,
adrift in some platonic trial balloon. He ran Delancey by
day and saw me at night; he doesn't need a lot of sleep.
John had this almost quaint, old Irish country approach to
marriage, the lifetime commitment, the sanctity of wedlock,
but I wanted to make sure that with me it just wasn't a
ninety-day glow. I don't dabble or play around, and I wasn't
someone John wanted to dabble with; he kept saying, "I
don't want to rush into bed and not have it work—it would
hurt too much." And for me, to go ahead and sleep with
someone would mean a real involvement, and I had some of
the same doubts about John that my husband had. I knew
he was charming, dynamic, but wasn't sure if he'd have
holding power for me because I come from a very tight
Jewish clan, highly traditionalized, old-fashioned—and I
like it, never rebelled against it like so many do. And John
seemed to do a lot of screwing around. All during our trial

period he was still openly sleeping with this square in the Delancey house, and he wasn't even being faithful to her. People would indict him in Games for being so offhand with her, cavalier, and he'd only shrug and say, "She bores me." Until John finally got sexually involved with me, he'd never been faithful to one woman in his life. Not running off to find other women he could screw, cut off one way of responding to women, which for John, might have been his *only* way. For one who works off his intuition as much as John, if the *feelings* aren't there, it won't work, like his marriage to Betty. In his mind, he knew the right thing would be to honor the marriage contract, but he didn't have those strong feelings for her, so he was bound to find other women to avoid making the marriage stick. The same with me, we're both strong about "doing the right thing," but if the right thing doesn't connect with your gut, it's a difficult problem, and that's what happened to my own marriage.

After eight months of seeing each other, we went to New York on a ten-day trip. This was the first time we ever slept together, and it was wonderful. If we had gone to some motel in San Francisco, I would have frozen! When we got back home, John still shouldered this terrible guilt, like he'd stolen me, which according to his way of thinking, he did, and he acted out his guilt in comical ways, insisting we pussyfoot around when everyone *knew* we were living together after the New York trip. We moved into this friend's apartment not far from Delancey, and would both go to work in the morning—by now I was on the Board of Directors—and John would say, "Walk into the house ten minutes after I do, better we aren't seen coming in together." And I'd yell at him, "Don't you see how *crazy* this is?" He was terrified the house wouldn't approve, saying, "Who is this square?" which was totally irrational, because ethically he couldn't get involved with a patient-resident."

Finally, the house called a Game on us where all John's

friends smiled indulgently and said, "Look, everyone knows about you and Mimi, and we're delighted. What are you tiptoeing around for?" I joined in the indictment, telling him that when you act furtive, you make something look wrong, even when there isn't. John admitted it was stupid of him. Then he called a Game and announced his decision to bring me into the house to live with him. It was a very hard thing for him to do.

My husband was staying with the twins, and I was running back to Berkeley three days a week to see them. Most of my guilt centers around the children. With my husband and the Delancey people, we did it straight and clean, but I still felt guilt about the twins. They're living now with John and me, and John is outstanding with them, a real doting father, roughhouse, piggyback, the whole route.

Perhaps I feel a twinge of guilt about my parents because they're unhappy about me, an only child, God's perfect jewel, getting a divorce and taking up with a gentile. They haven't met John, but saw him on a TV talk show and were impressed, especially Mama, being a spunky old radical herself. She didn't mind his drug and prison background, but couldn't get over his not being Jewish.

Besides loving John, I admire him for the way he handles our relationship, never arguing about my outside work. People have asked me if his old *macho* street attitude is changed, and I honestly don't know, because when we first went together it was total seclusion and I didn't observe him with other people. But those who knew John in the old days tell me he's utterly changed his attitude about women.

CHESTER STERN (a ten-year resident and top director of Synanon until he moved to Delancey): Mimi's a fantastic catalytic agent to John. She's brought out another side of John I never saw in the old Synanon days, a compassionate and creative side. When I first met him, he'd just come to

Synanon, and I found him holed up in the basement surrounded by psychology books. I knew after listening to this twenty-two-year-old kid that he was kind of smart, with plenty of potential, but somehow there were vital parts missing. Ten years later, one of the reasons I decided to stay in Delancey after I broke with Synanon, was that after my talks with John, he seemed to have hooked up his circuitry. He's grown up, come into his own, and I'm sure Mimi added something essential to his life and work. She's innovative, a strong woman, and we need that around here, because let's face it, it's going to take years before our women can build the confidence that will overcome the old *macho* mentality. But besides being tough and brilliant, she's so beautiful and warm, and a delight to be around, and she's made John a lot more fun to hang out with.

Mimi's flair for dealing with top government brass was helpful in soothing the State Department and Egyptian Consular Corps during the touchy negotiations over the Arabian mansion. She conceived the program of busing slum kids to Alcatraz and sold the idea to the National Park Service. She oversees the daily operations of the entire Foundation, but feels her most important work is to build the Explorers Department to re-educate addicts and prepare them for life on the outside.

MIMI SILBERT: I've got a difficult position here. Although I'm the executive director, a "co-president" in essence, the natural response of people is to think of my main role as John's woman. People's guts in Delancey Street are not attuned to women bosses, even though we've put women in many department head positions. There's still this big *macho* hangover from the street, and this is what I'm determined to change. Also, having two heads of anything is difficult. Sharing is not John's natural style, he's used to doing things on his own and this has been hard for us. He *wants* to share, but doesn't do it easily.

When I first came here, it was to apply for a NIMH

grant for $1 million. I decided not to because, even though
federal funding doesn't hold *that* many strings, at that stage
in Delancey's growth, any large funding would have been
disastrous. There is an entirely different psychology when
you *feel* the government is funding you, especially for huge
amounts, than when you feel you're supporting yourself. We
can't take foundation money for the running of the house,
food, maintenance, because it's critical to Delancey's program of self-reliance that our people know they're really
needed, that the money they bring in from the moving
company and the terrarium business is crucial to keep us
going. Otherwise they'd be engaged in work-therapy, which
has never worked. In Delancey there's a continual and unconscious push toward success because our *lives* depend on
the money we make.

This has led to a comic reversal, with some foundation
executives trying to convince us to take their money, telling
us, "You people are awfully close-minded about accepting
our money. Let us send you some data to persuade you it
won't be all that compromising." Still, I didn't go for it.
Large foundations are interested in research and their criteria
for determining success is very different from ours. I have
written proposals to small private foundations for very
limited forms of grants in two areas:

First, an initial capital outlay for a self-generating business, like the moving company, and that's the end of the
grant. I wrote a proposal for a few moving trucks, which we
purchased with the grant money. The same for the construction and auto-repair businesses, with the money going
strictly to training schools, not into the Delancey kitty as
a whole.

Second, community service projects, like senior citizens,
jail programs, court liaisons, with absolutely no strings attached to the money, which goes to our ex-cons and ex-
addicts to provide services to other oppressed groups in the
community.

I am also thinking toward possible grants in the future to set up additional corporations to become an educational institution. Because Delancey is a total commitment program, there's a lot of people we don't get to help because they, often rightfully, don't feel the need for two full years of Delancey, and they don't get anything else because the entire halfway house system nationwide is mostly a flop. Some are in jail for political reasons, like David Harris, others need help in getting jobs, others can't get paroled unless they have a halfway house to go to, not for two years, but for six months to get used to the community again. So we plan to broaden Delancey by setting up halfway houses that *work*, houses to deal with particular problems, like alcoholism. These future directions are open for grants.

Maher grudgingly accepts the small no-strings grants that Mimi Silbert arranged, but remains suspicious of the power of large foundation or government funds to corrupt the movement.

JOHN MAHER: If Pontius Pilate had been a smart Washington politician instead of a dumb Roman bureaucrat, he could have subverted the entire Christian movement by giving the Founder five thousand dinars to start a boy's club in Bethlehem to see how many Samaritans He could cure. Next year, the Carpenter would come back to Pilate to refund the grant because the new state regulations say they need two psychiatric social workers, one probation officer, and a fire escape. This would have cleverly diverted the Leader from His central purpose: to sit around with a dozen buddies and "work out a philosophy that's acceptable to us." Now, that's powerful talk, because if that ethic makes them feel good, lots more folks will join them.

Chuck Dederich insists it takes at least five years to clean up addicts before they can assume major roles in running Synanon. Mimi Silbert is working to get addicts back on the street in thirty months through a radical new program that

*prepares the patient to live on the outside in gradual steps,
like one of Jacques Cousteau's divers going through carefully
measured stages of decompression before surfacing. Late in
1974, she set up the Immigration Department to accustom
addicts to their first ninety days in the house.*

MIMI SILBERT: It's like coming to a new country where
all your old ways of thinking and talking are obsolete. The
Immigration Department concentrates on the newcomer,
teaching him to walk a new walk and talk a new talk. We
flip values around to their opposites. People coming through
our door tend to blame other people, their family, or society
for everything bad that's happened to them. We flip it to
the other extreme. It's all on them. Stealing is no longer a
sign of toughness. It's silly and weak. Working hard is no
longer a bag for squares to crawl into, it's looked up to. We
point out that while they were tricking off the people they
stole from, or were whores for, they themselves were the
real tricks because they ended in the joint with no money
and no friends.

But the most difficult stage comes after our people have
been here thirty months or so, when their behavior and
values are now anticriminal instead of antisocial. To make it
out in the community, they have to face the real horror we
are all grappling with, that most decisions are not clearly
either right or wrong, but a balance. What's right for the
kids and family may be wrong for me. What's right for me
may be wrong for my job.

To break this either-or pattern, I set up the Explorers,
who now number nearly a hundred. Their concentration is
on the process of decision making, which they must do themselves, rather than have someone do it for them. The Explorers learn in action how to balance values and find which
combinations suit the individuals' own situation. This is
hard, because up 'til now, the emphasis had always been on
right *behavior*. Now we tell them it's important to look at

the *process* of deciding what action to take, and there's no one right answer. It's a new and exciting stage in preparing to graduate. Most of our people, no matter what they do, or how well, feel in their gut that being here is not an *option*, that they came here as patients and can't make it on the outside. Graduation is thought of as a major step and they fear it. In here they've got jobs, their bills are paid, if they want a TV, they sign a requisition and get one from our warehouse, but outside is a whole new ball game. We're aiming to find ways to keep the place fluid, come in for a year, leave for a year, so that people can learn to deal with the *boredom* of the outside, because in Delancey every minute is programmed and John keeps the place rocking with holidays, entertainments. You are constantly barraged with activity here, so that when you go out, you're socked with the reality of generating things to do for yourself. That's one of the hardest problems of living outside. The Explorers are looking into ways for people to feel they can always belong here, but still have the option for different life-styles.

We want to end the Synanon either-or environment: either you're a patient or a big shot. Barbara Stern came here from Synanon and had the same battle with Delancey because she's capable of making her own decisions. Delancey either treated her as a patient, which is ridiculous for someone of her experience and maturity, or they flipped to the other extreme where she's a big shot in the upper eschelons and no one can tell her anything. And the reality of life is not either-or. Even if you're healthy, your friends yell at you, and people like John Maher need advice too. Synanon was so involved with the survival of the group that all the people simply had to fit in. Any commune becomes very norm-oriented and Delancey has to guard against this happening. The constant focus of the Explorers is to keep diversity alive.

CHAPTER NINE

Re-education

*"People quickly learn that the interests of all
oppressed groups—ghetto blacks, hard-hats, poor Southern
whites, even women and gays—are identical."*

Delancey Street's spartan re-education of immigrants derives from Synanon. On their first day, the men's heads are shaved to discourage any immediate notions of running home, and to blow their image as big-time hustlers. The first weeks of grimy kitchen work are calculated to humiliate con artists and silk-suited studs. During immigration, whose length varies to fit individual needs, they can see no visitors, nor contact anyone outside the house, especially their family, whose classic response to Delancey tends to encourage flight with anxious plaints of, "What are they doing to my poor baby in that terrible place?" Maher aims to build a new clan loyalty unfettered by old family ties. Sometimes these outside distractions are not mothers and fathers, but guitars and trumpets.

BARBARA STERN (Maher's secretary and head of the Game Club): For the addict-musician, his instrument is often more than a means of artistic expression, but an escape from people and responsibilities, and a constant reminder of the drug life. For this reason they must put music aside for their crucial first ninety days, so that all their time and energies can be funneled into making human contacts in this strange new environment. Once immigrants have reached that cut-off point when basic training is over, they are free to take up music again, and encouraged to use their talent to liven things up around the house.

Immigrants, in Games and out, are encouraged to reshape their identities as men and women, and to reject the machismo of the old street life. Maher is adamant that none of the vulnerable young women are sexually misused by the residents, especially the staff.

JOHN MAHER: When these women come to us for help, most of them have been used and don't even know it. No one with authority in the Foundation—male or female—can sleep with someone who comes to us for help until these inmates have been taught to regard themselves as human beings and not just a piece of meat, and have gone through our re-educative process to where they are no longer dependent on us, socially or economically. This is *not* going to be another of those freak free university professors-ball-students bullshit in the name of liberation. One of my staff broke this rule and I was ruthless—I just threw the son-of-a-bitch *out!*

Nearly half of Delancey's population is black. The rest is largely Chicano, urban Irish and Italian, and Southern white. Their racial re-education begins the days they enter.

JOHN MAHER: When newcomers arrive here, they tend to isolate themselves, black with black, white with white, because they come from neighborhoods and prisons where a childish form of racism is encouraged. When this happens, it means that these victims' sense of self-identity had been destroyed and that they must take on the identity of their ethnic or geographic group. We break these groups up. Their previous experiences with other people and groups have been almost totally negative. The key is to handle people the same. As they emerge back into society, they learn that racism is foolish and that the interests of ethnic groups are closely related to those who shared the same experiences— drugs, poverty, and oppression. They learn here that their freedoms are interdependent, that there is no freedom for one without freedom for all. When blacks and whites understand this concept, they are truly integrated.

Delancey Street is the only organization of this kind that involves itself in questions that affect the black community *outside* our own group, so that militant blacks don't have to feel they've sold out when they come here. We fought the Nazi party on the school board, helped poor blacks get their food stamps, helped the Black Panther schools, and our blacks prevented the racists from bombing the Urban League, which gave Delancey an award for fighting oppression. So Delancey offers the ethnic minority, hard-hat as well as black, a platform to fight for their people.

When we get white red-neck racists in here, the old whites take them aside and explain certain fundamental realities—that for years the whites and blacks have been kept in a state of chronic war and denied justice by the system and its administrators, and that as long as we continue to fight each other, we can't get ahead. When this begins to make sense, we do something simple—we tell them the truth, which a racist environment never does; we tell them that whites and blacks have been used as scapegoats for each other on the lowest levels, encouraged by the government and the bureaucracy, and that the interests of ghetto blacks, hard-hats, and poor Southern whites are identical.

We show them that the hard-hat nuts and the young black revolutionaries are the same phenomenon, but are looking at the cut from different sides. When Archie Bunker screams, "I'm tired of gettin' mugged, and I'm gonna break some jaws," it's the same thing as the black radicals saying, "Get these corrupt cops, dope pushers, and creep social workers out of my neighborhood!" Because of the difference in political rhetoric and their sociological platform, they've got different perspectives. But the good people in *both* these camps find themselves at war with each other, when they're actually on the same side, and in this kind of struggle, it's only the giant bureaucracies that win.

Quickly we find that the most virilent white racists can begin to respect blacks who stand up for themselves, and that when blacks meet really *tough* whites for the first time, instead of middle-class social worker lames, a mutual respect builds to where they can work together. The toughest gangsters are *verbally* more racist when they come here, and racist in terms of who they hang out with. But the tougher they are, the more quickly they will grant respect to a member of another ethnic group who behaves in a fashion acceptable to their code.

So the toughest whites and blacks can very quickly integrate and work together. It's the weaklings, the whiners, the ones who need their own group around them to support their deflated egos who are the slowest to integrate.

In Games, a white racist is talked down to, laughed at, and maybe yelled at from time to time. We find it silly, some asshole comes here of *any* color, never done anything except steal off his mother, pimp off his wife, sell dope to poor people—this clown gets up and says, "I don't like Armenians, they're oily, smell weird, and got the brain-pans of salamanders." This is comical, but *not* in a threatened environment where the integration is not genuine, and where such nonsense is greeted with horror. But in Delancey Street, we greet this kind of garbage with great gales of laughter. How can some black dope peddler come in here, selling heroin to black children to keep them enslaved for the benefit of the landlords and the police structure, actually get up and rail at the white oppressor? He *is* the fucking oppressor! We recognize that racist babble and drug use are merely the symptomology of the oppressed, therefore not great crimes.

The way to integrate in the United States is the way we do it here—you start at the *top*. We do not ask some poor new nut who just arrived here from Little Italy to embrace all the Irish; we put a black man or woman on our Board of Directors and tell them, "Whatever you want to do for your community, we stand with you." What happens is that the people at the top dispense jobs, patronage, have respect, and are *visibly* integrated, so that becomes the thing for newcomers on the lower echelons to do.

But what they do in America is to enforce integration on the *bottom*. In Boston, there's a township called Winchester that doesn't want to integrate, got a lot of money and Mafia in it. Then there's South Boston, where nobody got past the eighth grade. The powers that be did not choose to integrate Winchester first, where this could be done very easily, and set an example for South Boston, which they chose to integrate first, because the bastards knew that there, the poorest elements would immediately feel threatened, insecure, and fight each other, tying up *real* integration for another ten years with endless lawsuits.

That's why we teach *all* history at Delancey Street. Black history is not a topic for black children, but for all Americans. Since a large chunk of black, labor, and women's history never filtered through the public school system, our decision-making powers were based on false premises. We urge our blacks not to get hung up on past injustices like the I.R.A., which is forever crying, "They killed Wolfe Tone," but to ask, "What do we want for our children?" We encourage blacks to look to the future, not to whine, "You honkies owe me four hundred years back wages." Most movements have to go through these childish phases, which is why so many have failed. In America this kind of bullshit is encouraged because it isolates the black and white leadership from any concerted action—they all get hot and resent each other, like the blacks in SNCC and CORE in the sixties wanting to exclude whites, and elements in the black movement putting down Martin Luther King as an Uncle Tom. The establishment *loves* all this bullshit.

Here, we teach people that labor and capital in this country was written on the backs of black slaves, white miners, and Chinese coolies, and that there is really no difference between them when it comes to the intention of the exploiters. Once our people grasp this essential truth, they are no longer children to be manipulated and tricked off against each other by the establishment, but can begin to do what *all* responsible, law-abiding citizens do—register with the political party of their choice, vote, organize, demonstrate, agitate, demand control of their destinies—and throw the bums *out!*

CHAPTER TEN

The Graduate

*"We're not a monastary where novitiates only
have contact with those already converted."*

If boring from within establishment politics is
the right arm of the revolution, the left arm is the Explorers
program. Maher and Dr. Silbert aim to put ex-addicts out in
the field where they can proselytize.

JOHN MAHER: We're always told, "You don't cure as
many as you should." Of course not. We are the Harvard
of drug programs, not the City College. We are grooming
tough and intelligent leaders to go into unions, city politics,
businesses, and religions, to change those institutions. We're
not interested in curing addict kids so they can go back to
the slums, swallow methadone, drink wine, and go on
welfare.

MIMI SILBERT: Urging residents to get involved politi-
cally with the community, and placing our people in jobs
on the outside will keep us from repeating Synanon's inward-
directed mistakes. We're not a cloistered order whose members' only contacts are others who are already converted.

Long before Dr. Silbert set up the Explorers, Ken Hepper
became the first graduate, living and working outside while
playing Games and advising would-be graduates on the emotional problems of living away from the house. Hepper's last

crime was a stick-up to support his habit. When the victim turned out to be a plain-clothes cop, they sent him to Nevada State Prison, where Synanon ran an experimental program. On release, he moved into Synanon for two years before coming to Delancey Street, staying thirty months before graduation, working outside for six months before making the final break of finding his own apartment.

KEN HEPPER: Honeywell, Incorporated, decided to hire me after an interview that lasted from 9:30 A.M. into late afternoon. I convinced them I was going to be a field engineer in the computer industry whether they hired me or not. I learned in Games how to handle myself in a job interview. I used to be the kind of person who, if I was standing in line behind a guy who was standing on my foot, I'd either suffer in silence or try to kill him. Games taught me an alternative; I could tap him on the shoulder and say, "Hey, you're on my foot." As a condition of my employment, Honeywell did not permit me to talk about my background for the first six months on the job. Being an ex-con had been my badge, or excuse. I had to be accepted or rejected as Ken Hepper, computer engineer. When I graduated, Delancey's Credit Union helped me with a loan to rent an apartment and buy a car. Later, when some of my family needed financial help, they came through with another loan.

*Head of the Credit Union (CU) and "barber" * for an advanced group of residents working toward graduation, is Mary Ayres, a middle-aged Mother Superior of quiet dignity and brisk business expertise. After ten years of addiction to barbiturates, she moved into Synanon in 1963 for seven years, heading Santa Monica's Finance Office and running the Detroit house with her then husband Tim.*

MARY AYRES: By 1971, I felt I got from Synanon what I went for, and left to see if I could make it on my own. I

* Delancey Street slang for a group leader.

made it the hard way: $10 cash, no job, three thousand miles from home. That's why I eventually got interested in the Credit Union, because it provided a financial cushion for graduates. When I left Synanon, I didn't know John had started his own house. I heard about Delancey, paid a visit, and stayed, living in, but on a work-out for 2½ years as secretary to the manager of the Bechtel Corporation in Oakland.

In November 1974, Maher asked Ayres to take over the Credit Union, founded a year earlier when Billy Maher went to see the head of the National Credit Union Association in San Francisco, Thomas Scrobert. He became wired to the idea of ex-convicts establishing credit, although everyone in his office told him it wouldn't work. Scrobert said he was going to make it work if he had to run it himself.

MARY AYRES: Scrobert really went to bat for us, and we got our CU charter in September 1973. Today our assets are $30,000. We're an unusual CU, not limited to Delancey residents, but open to anyone who wants to invest at $5.00 a share. It has a future as a very profitable business. At present, we ask investors to keep their money in at least six months, because the request for loans is higher than our reserves. A lot of outside investors have put up money, not just because we're a social movement, but because we are competitive in the investment field, paying 5½ percent interest, and this rate is going up. We granted loans to one private investor and three graduates. A new Board of Directors came in early in 1975 to fit the changing picture of the CU, which had been run by residents, but the new Board includes people from the finance world—manager of the Wells Fargo branch where Delancey does all its banking, the CU manager for the A.A.A. [American Auto Association] and Vincent Hallinan, a well-known San Francisco attorney.

My fuction as "barber" for potential graduates is interrelated to my job with the CU. This group of thirty men and women has been here at least eighteen months, and proved themselves responsible. The difference between my group and the others is, I don't make their decisions for them. They have tremendous freedom, can go away on weekends. I'm not interested who they're seeing, they don't sign in. I tell them, "I trust you, don't make me look bad, because I got an image and don't like to be dumped on," and usually they don't let me down. Being the only woman "barber," I get some *machismo* problems, but not as much as a younger woman would. They relate to me as a mother figure. I don't like it much, but there it is. I'm not one for raising my voice, so when I do, they know it's serious. After all I've been through, I find it difficult to be truly angry. My potential graduates get $20 a month walking-around money, which, if they choose, I invest for them in the CU. When I give my people their Credit Union book, most of them look at it with awe and say, "Gee, I never in my life had a bank book before!" It's something to see.

CHAPTER ELEVEN

Fun and Games

"A Game is like an orgasm—
just words until you've had the experience."

To fend off institutional boredom and orphan-
age pall, Maher and his staff keep Delancey jumping with
picnics, outings, sports, holidays, fairs, dances, and even foreign travel. Two-month-long trips to Mexico were set up by
San Francisco attorney-archeologist Vincent Hallinan, whose
itinerary by-passed the tourist traps of Acapulco for the ruins
of Monte Alban and the Yucatan. A group of residents made
an African safari. An Explorers' Club sends ghetto youngsters
on rafting trips down California rivers. "There's no greater
joy in life," said Maher, "then to watch tough, big-city gangsters terrified by their first encounter with a garter snake."
Afro-Cuban jazz stars Cal Tjader, Tito Puente, Willie Bobo,
and Mongo Santamaria play frequent concerts in the house.
The Delancey Street football squad bested the Police and
Fire Department teams, only to be squashed by the Gay
Liberation eleven, "all over six foot three," said Maher, "and
very rough."

Christmas and Thanksgiving are lavishly celebrated, but
the most festive occasions are the Jewish holidays, another
holdover from Synanon. The Seder supper to observe Passover is Delancey's event of the year, with five hundred

yarmulka-wearing residents and friends joining the rabbi in readings from the Hebrew prayer book, chanting traditional passover songs, followed by a black choir intoning "Go Down, Moses" and the playing of Martin Luther King's "I Have a Dream." The Seder is climaxed with huge servings of kosher chicken and matzoh-ball soup.

The Annual Black History Week features lectures, films, readings from Langston Hughes, Nikki Giovanni, and Malcolm X, followed by a soul dinner of fried chicken, cornbread, black-eyed peas, collard greens, and sweet potato pie.

Improving the food is an obsession, and nothing will enrage Delancey's staff more than the sight of a sloppy kitchen.

BILLY MAHER: Almost all prison riots start in the mess hall, and probably most family fights, too. Food and sex are such visceral things that it's very rough to fuck with them, and since we have to have certain restrictions on sex around here, with men outnumbering women four-to-one, the least we can do is give our people a good meal.

Breakfast is followed by a morning meeting, conducted by residents, taking turns.

Good morning, people—how're you feeling this morning? (Loud applause.) Feel like you going to take on the world this morning? (Prolonged whistles and yells.) Now people, we got a big weekend ahead of us—the Valentine's Day Party, the demonstration and march for the Farm Workers Union, and Black History Week, so there's no excuse for some of you laying around your rooms watching some dumb-ass program on TV.

I got an announcement: You got to stop leaving lights on and radios running when you leave your rooms. It's just this kind of irresponsible bullshit that has kept us down all these years, and we can't be running up our light bills this way. Are there any other announcements?

MARY NUTTER: Some of us have been wasting food, picking at the meat and leaving the vegetables. If you don't want something, please tell the waiter when you are served.

BOB TRULL (head of the warehouse at Pier 41): You new people should know that we've got a good overflow of anything you need at the warehouse, and all you have to do is come down, sign a proper requisition, and get clothes, shoes, radios, some good TV sets in working order, household appliances, and plenty of good magazines, *New Yorker*, *Newsweek*, and not old stuff, either, recent issues. So come down and pick up what you need. To close the meeting, has anyone got a thought for today? Sue? Let's give her a hum. (Loud humming.)

SUE MCFADDEN: I cried because I had no shoes, and then I met a man who had no feet. (Wild applause.)

Dinner consumes a chatty, table-hopping ninety minutes, enlivened perhaps by a strolling guitarist, wedding announcement, or a surprise birthday cake for a recent immigrant, probably his first.

Once dishes are cleared, a hum of anticipation signals the approach of Games, Delancey's favorite amusement and means of letting-go. There's an all-Jewish Game, Games for children, barbers (tribe leaders), and the Friday Night Minion [1] Game each resident must play with a static, unvarying group of twenty. Some Games are called by request: A black social worker is spoiling to get in a Game with a "letterhead liberal" who exacts sky-high rent for his rundown ghetto flats. A young lawyer is startled to find himself in a Game with a former client who indicts him for malpractice. One of Delancey's construction crew calls a Game on his boss for "fucking over me on the job." As a coveted reward for hard work, business incentive, role modeling to newcomers, and creative Game playing, residents are honored with invi-

---

1. Minion: a quorum of ten required to hold a Jewish religious service.

tations to the weekly Board of Directors Game with Maher, Mimi Silbert, Tom Grapshi, Mon Sandhu, and their square business advisors, Hal Fenton and Dick Kirschman.

Maher might still find time to call out the Games as in the early days. To ease the pre-Game tension that grips new players, and even some old hands, he works the afterdinner crowd like a circus barker and Catskill comic, clanging out a mixture of in-house gossip and vaudeville gags, announcing the bar mitzvah of the black chef, and profane abuse of whatever government is around, couched in the accents of the street punk, the case-heavy social worker, the Madison Avenue wiseacre, the bored suburban housewife dabbling in group sex.

Maher shuffles residents and squares into several groups of about fifteen, although when enough Game rooms are available, he prefers twelve—"Two thousand years ago, the Carpenter found a dozen to be a good, workable number." He's careful to mix parole officers with ex-cons, jeweled matrons with black whores, teen-agers with grandparents, hard-hats with English teachers.

The week before going into their first encounter, squares attend Game Club orientation where ground rules are explained by Barbara Stern, a Synanon veteran with eleven years of Game-playing. She's aided by Jack Webb, a craggy, handsome "black Irishman" who spent eighteen years as police inspector before heading his own firm that handled security for the 1974 Hearst Food Giveaway. Awed by Delancey's role in salvaging this program that had been given up as hopeless, Webb became "totally involved in all facets of Delancey Street."

Before orientation, Stern screens the newcomers, asking how many have ever been seriously involved in drugs. This former boss dope fiend claims she can spot them even before they raise their hands. After the meeting, she asks them about the extent of their habit, how long they've been

clean, using her gut reaction to decide if they should come
in as residents, if they are conning, and if they can be trusted
around the house. Some can play Games next week; others
are gently told to come back in another six months.

Orientation in El Portel's plush restaurant-lounge starts
with the showing of a twenty-minute documentary on Delancey, filmed as a segment of the CBS "Sixty Minutes" TV
series, with Maher's fireball delivery punctuated with discreet
bleeps to pacify the Federal Communications Commission.

When the lights go up, Jack Webb recounts the history
of Delancey before getting into what most newcomers have
come to hear—what to expect when they walk into a Game.

JACK WEBB: These are basic encounter sessions. Some of
these people in Games might be working in our Union Street
restaurant. Where on the outside, a waiter might harbor
murderous thoughts about the maitre d' for weeks on end,
with no outlet for his feelings, here, he can vomit out all his
animosities and frustrations.

BARBARA STERN: We want our residents to relate to people like you, to know what it means to be respectable, to
hold down a job five days a week, because most of our people
have never held any job more than six months. Our outside
people who play Games here find it exciting, perhaps the
most meaningful experience of their lives. Games are set up
so there's always some people in the house with many years
of Game experience playing with you. When I first came to
Synanon eleven years ago, I didn't like Games, didn't understand them, or why everyone was yelling at each other. Then
I began to find out that the Game was what made the house
run, where business was conducted, people re-educated; it
was what kept us clean, kept physical violence out of our
lives. So I started to play Games every chance I got to overcome my initial fear.

If you've been in group encounters, you'll find our Games
different, they're leaderless, though at times, the strongest

person in the room will assume control. It's not a spectator sport. You won't enjoy them if you try to sit back and watch. Jump in and talk. Force yourself to say one thing to everyone the Game is on. The worst thing that can happen is you'll be told to fuck off.

Don't defend someone the Game is on, because one of the reasons for the Game is to learn how to defend yourself. If Jack Webb and I are in a Game, and I'm getting the shit kicked out of me and he jumps to my defense, I'm really mad at Jack. We call them bleeding hearts, and a lot of players will sympathize with someone under attack, and over-react.

JACK WEBB: If you *didn't* sympathize, you'd have to be a heartless prick, because you'll hear all kinds of things said to others that you'll identify with.

BARBARA STERN: We don't ask for anything like a three-month committment to Games. We ask you to play a few Games and then join a tutorial which is a form of Game, but mainly it cuts up what happens in Games, where you can ask questions and talk about your feelings and experiences in Games. Then you can go back to regular Games armed with a little information. We have what we call the Neighborhood, which *does* have a leader, a static Game with the same people on a four-week committment, so when you come down here, you know some people and make good friends. There's an entertainer's Game—it started with a rock group that couldn't get to the gig on time, lots of internal bickering; after a few months of Games, the band really got it together and cooks well.

JACK WEBB: Some house rules: On the day you play your Game, we want you to come here fairly clear, nothing to drink, no pot. Lot of our kids are only a month or two away from the street—they can smell pot fourteen blocks away, on your clothes, in your hair. We don't want anything to trigger them off, give them ideas about wandering out.

You young ladies in the room should be aware that we have 150 sex fiends wandering around this insane asylum. You walk by them, think they're cute, and start wiggling your ass, immediately, they're going to assume you're madly in love with them. You're tampering with a very touchy commodity. We do not discourage friendships, but if you find yourself developing an interest in one of our men, talk to his barber and find out what gives. We got some kid in here only a few months, he goes ga-ga over you and sticks up the gas station down the street to buy you a diamond.

BARBARA STERN: What Jack just said is *very* important. There aren't enough women to go around here. Many of our guys have been in prison a long time. When they're here about a year they have permission to date square Game Club players. So it's not unusual for a new woman to walk in her first night and have three or four guys hit on her immediately. We try to discourage this. If you've been here playing Games for thirty days and fall madly in love with one of our dope fiends, *please* come and talk to somebody about it, because some of our guys are real smooth-talking cons. On the other hand, some have had long and *good* relationships with members of our Game Club. But come to us first about it, or you may get in trouble.

JACK WEBB: You women can always tell our newcomers —their heads are shaved. We urge you to avoid them. You men, if you want to come in and rap with our immigrants, great. They need this kind of attention, being very insecure when they first come here. Any questions?

Will new Game players get beaten up bad? Do you tend to take it easy on beginners?

BARBARA STERN: Games aren't as brutal as you must have heard. Nobody leaves a Game smashed without getting patched up. Our people are *concerned* about other people. Being called a dirty bitch isn't all that terrible, it's just words. You'll find here there's basic folk wisdom in children's sayings like "sticks and stones may break my bones . . ." In Games you can mirror yourself on fifteen different people, see yourself as others see you. That doesn't mean it's all valid. If you think some of it's good stuff, you can work on it. If some of it's bullshit, it doesn't matter, because a Game is truly a *game.*

You don't take your anger *out* of a Game; that's really a discipline. I can go into a Game, angry at something that happened at work, and beat hell out of someone for something silly, like the shoes they're wearing, and my anger has absolutely *nothing* to do with my feelings about that person. Then the Game gets on me and everybody says, "Say, what the hell's wrong with *you* tonight?" Here, all this emotional garbage gets dumped. The Game is not therapeutic. If you're ill, and think you have deep psychological problems, don't come in here looking to be cured.

Do you think the Game is universally good for everyone?

BARBARA STERN: We want to emphazise that Games are *not* for everyone. If someone calls you a stupid asshole in a Game and leaves you utterly smashed, and you take this home and brood about it all week, and take this bad feeling back with you in Game after Game, then Games are not for you.

How do you make sure there's privacy in a Game, that what you say won't get all over town?

BARBARA STERN: We can't make certain that some people won't blab about what was said in Games, but we do encourage a private morality by emphasizing in Games, "You can say anything you want in here, because it won't get outside."

Do you encourage people to be open and honest outside of Games?

BARBARA STERN: Open and friendly, yes. Open and hostile, no. If someone fucks over me on the floor, that is, outside the Game, I don't return the hostility, but would request to be in a Game with that person, where I get *good* and hostile!

If you're feeling unusually vulnerable on the day of your Game—your wife left you, or you lost your job, or are feeling suicidal, should you seek out a Game, or avoid it?

JACK WEBB: This is *exactly* the best time to play your Game. A man might go in and find it boring after ten minutes and say, "Look, I got some pretty heavy things I want to talk about tonight. I want to blow my brains out, but instead I come over to talk to you guys . . ."

Mr. Webb, I notice you keep stressing men and guys. Are they in that much of a dominant position around here?

JACK WEBB: That's my chauvinistic background showing.

BARBARA STERN: And do we ever talk to him about this in Games—*all* the time!

There's rarely enough time in orientation to cover actual Game technique, which includes the use of exaggeration and ridicule to break down an image. A middle-aged Don Juan with a habit of hugging young women on the floor might be accused of attempted rape. The indictment may be trivial or absurd; the response is all that matters. If the target defends itself against any attack, no matter how extreme or engrossed, players will be quick to point this out. If the target then overcompensates by not responding at all, the group may grow doubly abusive. A woman coming to Games in blue jeans and no make-up may be indicted for sloppiness and showing disrespect to the group. If she returns next week all gussied-up, she may be attacked for looking like a painted two-bit whore. How she handles these contradictory charges can reveal to the group, and to herself, much about her responses to her job, family, and friends.

Players who instinctively raise their guard when under attack can often be hit by a carom shot cued by an expert: For two murderous hours, the Game has been on Harold, who sighs with relief when the group shifts its attack to his wife Martha. The player setting up the carom shot will deliver a withering indictment, seemingly aimed at Martha, but actually directed at husband Harold, whose guard is now relaxed. If the shot is true, unwary Harold will react, either verbally, or with some facial or body gesture not lost on the group. People with a lifelong habit of not listening to, or looking at others, after a few months of Games find themselves studying patterns of speech, dress, and behavior.

Skilled players are quick to spot when they are being "tossed a bone." A wealthy socialite came to Games claiming to be an alcoholic. Suspicious, the group urged him to take the booze test devised by the Yale Clinic of Alcoholic Studies. If he could drink one ounce of hard liquor—no more and no less—everyday for thirty consecutive days, he was not an alcoholic. He passed the test easily, since he was not a drunk, but only used this as a guise to avoid talking about problems he was too ashamed to discuss. Alcoholism was a bone he tossed to the group, which tossed it back to the target, who then began to open up about deeper problems, like his sexual impulses toward small boys.

One advantage of Games over one-to-one psychotherapy is that players can be observed in a variety of social situations. Like many psychiatrists, George's doctor made it a rule never to socialize with his patients. It took the Game less than a month to find out what the psychiatrist never learned in five years—that five-foot George always picked wives and women friends who were at least a head taller.

After players develop skills in these three-to-five-hour encounters, they may be asked to join Dissipations, marathon weekend Games beginning on Friday evening when players already have a full working day's fatigue behind them. Players with severe image problems, whose defenses cannot be broken in shorter Games, have experienced startling breakthroughs under massive group attack after two sleepless days. Stick-up men slobber helplessly, pinstriped dignitaries get holy-roller seizures, sedate matrons scream like fishwives. This carefully orchestrated long day's journey into night ends on Sunday afternoon with its participants hugging and kissing, wafting about in a state of benign euphoria.

BARBARA STERN: We found a way to have psychic visions, to get really high, without the chemicals; we don't need them.

CHAPTER TWELVE

Maher's Game

"You have witnessed a miracle here."

For John Maher, the Game is more than recreation. It is his tool for running a tight ship from the captain's deck to the scullery, a staff meeting where employeremployee beefs are aired, where new business and real-estate plans are tested.

Games show a side of Maher not seen in seminars, lectures, or what passes for casual conversation. Since engrossment is a common Game technique, everything about Maher seems exaggerated in Games. His sarcasm is monstrous, his rages frightening, his mimicry so phonographic that he makes Games a turmoil of hysteria, tears, and howling laughter.

The Game that follows is not typical because Maher dominates the play, with much less give-and-take than is found in most Games. Here, Maher gives while the others take. No Game can be fully captured in print, because over a dozen players simultaneously respond with looks and gestures of such wealth and complication as to tax the descriptive powers of Tolstoy. Also, the following Game has been severely edited, since to reproduce its five hours of dialogue intact would run to volume length.

The Game was played in the summer of 1972 in the spacious living room of the now-vacated Arabian mansion. In addition to Maher, the players (whose names and occupations have been changed to avoid a violation of privacy) include:

King Kong, one of the few residents who never spent time in jail. This hulking, though gentle, former addict was in charge of Delancey's kitchen, and had been with the Foundation from the beginning.

Joanie Levin, a young, dark, and sexually provocative Jewish upper-class square, toying with the notion of moving into Delancey to get "really involved."

Harold Cook, thirty-five-year-old Synanon alumnus, ex-con, junkie, with plenty of street smarts and a crack salesman working in the Supply Department.

Stan Parkinson, young head of the Game Club and manager of a prosperous, mod clothing store. Before his involvement with Delancey, he led the life of a weekend hippie.

Ruth Parkinson, Stan's quiet, attractive wife, mother of their two children. She works full-time assisting Barbara Stern run the Game Club.

Slug Mozzarella, a semiliterate addict off the streets of New Jersey, who works in the machine shop and attends Delancey's high school.

Frank Farber, a successful real-estate broker who knew Maher in Synanon Games, and is a member of Delancey's Board of Directors.

Myron Baker, young San Francisco attorney, one of many that handle legal work for the Foundation and its people.

(Footnotes are used to explain Game technique.)

The Game opens with Maher's indictment of his cook, King Kong.

JOHN MAHER (very loud): You took your fat, lard ass away from the heat and responsibility of organizing a kitchen, sat around the house with the other fat lames, and when you came back, food was served in an atrocious manner! If this were a state prison, there'd be a fuckin' riot!

Unreal! A bunch of surly, acne-ridden whores throwing slop at guys who work their ass off to feed your fat ass! You don't feel *bad* about that?

KING KONG (softly): I didn't know what those guys were doing . . .

JOHN MAHER: Listen you Nazi bastard! Don't gimme any of them Eichmann lines! You would run a crew of ten new people, three of them just released from state hospitals! You would leave three psychopaths and seven kicking addicts hacking up rutabagas with machetes, and forget to go down and *check* on them once in a while? Did it ever occur to you to look in now and then to make certain one of these poor, crazed assholes didn't piss in the soup?

HAROLD COOK: When I went down to the kitchen last Sunday to see what was burning, like, the whole house thought the place was on fire, you literally threw me out of the kitchen, you fuckin' creep scum-bag!

JOHN MAHER: Can you handle this job? Last night, hundreds of people were milling around after being rudely treated by the people that work for you! (His voice drops to a whisper.) And what about that psychotic eleven-year-old child bride [1] who came to us looking for help—the one you were blopping up and down on? Did you feel any responsibility for tying her up and fucking with her mind?

KING KONG: John, since we broke up, I haven't bothered her at all. I don't feel . . .

JOHN MAHER: Now listen carefully, people, and you will learn something about the subhuman mind. You ask this fat fool, "Tell us what you feel," and he begins to tell us what he *doesn't* feel! Now that your penis has shrunk down and isn't pointing straight up anymore, do you feel an occasional

1. Typical engrossment. Kong's lover was actually nineteen, but the indictment is serious, since she came to Delancey, if not psychotic, in a disturbed state, and Kong, as a longtime resident, knew he was violating a rule against sexual involvement with newcomers.

pang when you see this child, that you might have impeded her progress?

KING KONG: Well, I didn't have an old lady the first year I was here, and had some sexual hang-ups, so I see this girl I liked, and we went together five months, and then broke up, so I don't see . . .

JOHN MAHER: So it's really all right to molest a child because you hadn't been laid in a year! Kong—everything you do begins with an excuse: the kitchen you befoul, this girl you pollute . . .[2]

MYRON BAKER (suddenly putting the Game on Slug Mozzarella): Get yourself another lawyer, Slug, I'm tired of this shit. This is the third time you've come to me for a divorce and then changed your mind. Why can't you cut this cunt loose, a woman who fucked all your friends, moved her mother into your house with her twenty-nine cats, drove you to desperate behavior, to using drugs, blackmailed you? A woman you shot at and deliberately missed? (Unlike the other players, Mozzarella dummies up, writhing in miserable silence.)

JOHN MAHER (very gently): Slug—why don't you do what you came here to do? Get a pair of balls? You keep this trouble bottled up inside you, and you'll wind up nuthouse bound, I've seen it happen. Or out on the street shooting dope again. Now it's very comforting for you to sit there and torture yourself, you big fucking baby. You got to clean all this shit up! Got to have some self-respect, and you can't get it, Slug, until you get rid of the broad. Do you still harbor fantasies she'll come back to you as a good wife? (Mozzarella nods mutely.) *Great!* Getting a divorce doesn't rule this out. If she wants to come back it will be on *your* terms,

2. Maher breaks off the indictment of King Kong, leaving him something to work on, his tendency for making excuses. Maher sees no reason to patch up Kong, who has been in Delancey long enough to patch himself up.

because you're a *man*. If you can't stand alone, she won't come back to you, Slug. You can't block it out any more, got to take a position. I divorced *my* wife in a great tangle of feelings, and I swear to Christ, she couldn't *stand* me. I hadn't divorced the bitch fifteen minutes, I can't get *rid* of her! It's a letter a week, and "Join me in Amsterdam," and "Why can't we be friends?" I tell you, Slug, divorce does *wonderful things* for a marriage! And what about your hostility toward women, Slug? What are you doing to work on that?

SLUG MOZZARELLA: I work on that alla time, John, I really do . . .

JOHN MAHER (quietly): No you don't, because you keep hanging onto the women that *feed* this hostility—the wife who fucked every St. Bernard that wandered in the house, the mother-in-law that spent all your money. We're not going to let you keep this all to yourself, Slug. We're going to make you open up and tell us what this cunt's got hanging over you . . .

(Maher abruptly turns to put the Game on Joanie Levin.) Here's this member of our service crew, with a rich, mockie, Jew-type father, supported her all her life, throwing her life away as a mattress. I have two dozen of my best men fucking you and your roommate at any given moment. Did *Reagan* pay you to come here? Did our Governor tell you to "go down to Delancey Street, fuck as many of them as possible, get them all jealous and upset—and bust Maher out of business?" Is this a plan like Watergate?

FRANK FARBER: The night of the Hallowe'en party, this dumb cunt comes up to me and says, "That fuckin' Eddie—last night he fucked me, and tonight he won't even speak to me." Now all our distinguished guests were here—rich people, politicos who could do us some good—and they *hear* this baby shit!

MYRON BAKER: Joanie—I'm curious. Just how many men

in this room *have* gotten into your pants? (Four men in the Game raise their hands, amid howls of laughter, goading the heretofore sullen Joanie into a piercing wail.)

JOANIE LEVIN: That's not fair, you motherfuckers! That's not *fair!*

JOHN MAHER (softly): Joanie—don't you think you're mildly inappropriate to go up to a middle-aged real-estate man you barely know, and bore him with the intimate details of your sex life? Suppose Frank's charming wife went around telling everyone, "Boy! did Frank give me a *terrific* bite on the clit last night!" What would you think? We don't really mind it, it's *fun,* this dilettante kid-shit of yours, and I'd encourage it if we weren't in Games, because it gets all the newcomers to come around, thinking, "Jesus, this Delancey Street is great—you get laid all the time!" But if you want to do something about *yourself,* dear, why don't you *stop* all this bullshit?

FRANK FARBER: I heard her say something she heard in a Game made her horny, "boy, I sure would like to get fucked." Now I figure any woman who advertises like that must be frigid, a real Frostie the Snow Lady.

JOHN MAHER: My, isn't she *lib*erated? Joanie—playing sex goddess around this loony bin is humiliating for you. Pathetic. You're degrading yourself. We're not trying to impede the free discussion of sex, but we *are* trying to take away your prop by which you get some very bad attention, dear. We don't like it in our house because it's bad for *you,* impaling yourself on one erect penile member after another. Makes you look like a camp follower. Makes you look as foolish as Stan Parkinson, here, flapping his wee-wee at every eleven-year-old groupie huddled in the corner of his hip, mod clothing store. (Louder.) Well, what about it Stan? A week ago we made you manager of the Game Club. What have you done about it?

STAN PARKINSON: John, you know I came in here a year

ago and took a pledge, made a committment. Well, it's crazy, because all last week the only thing I had on my mind was that my year was almost up. So last night I smoked the first joint I've had in a year.

JOHN MAHER (dangerously calm): That's *your* business. We don't care if our squares smoke pot, long as they don't do it on our premises and *do* talk about it in Games, like you—like some young lawyer can't get laid any other way, wants to signify to some Pan Am stewardess by buying oregano in North Beach and is puffing away in his Sausalito digs, *fine*. Long as we know about it. Because our people are going out into a world where dilettantes like you *do* things like this, and they better learn *here* how to handle this on the outside. You got to realize that an addictive personality would rather get high than anything in the world. He spots some jackoff like you toking away on weed at some Yuletide office party, and thinks, "If this guy can smoke a joint, and still drag down all that bread, why can't I?" So five weeks after he lights up, your ex-junkie's back on the needle! Every time, Stan!

FRANK FARBER: Why would you endanger this whole organization, six days after you were made manager of the Game Club? You, a role model for a lot of people around here?

JOHN MAHER: Well, Frank, you see it's back to groovy time for Stan.

HAROLD COOK (with more disgust than heat): Fuck this shit. I'm *tired* of having squares like this come down here, treated like the Pope, while I gotta break my balls in our Supply Department to make John Maher here *rich*. I wanna be treated *nice*, like this shithead who can be on our Board of Directors and smoke a joint. Throw the motherfuckin' creep out!

JOHN MAHER (raging at Stan, ignoring for the moment

Harold's carom shot about getting rich): I got fifty men here on *parole*, cocksucker! One judge offered to give me fifteen men out of the slammer, and [Sheriff] Hongisto'll give me another fifty, and one fuckin' punk like you, gets identified with us, gets busted like some dumb-ass rock guitar player, it jeopardizes a lot of lives! (In a whisper.) You think, "We're all alone in the car tonight, it's safe, I can toke a little weed." (Gently.) We've never been against it for squares, Stan. We *do* recommend that middle-aged motherfuckers like you going through their second childhood, until they get it under control, pass it by. Little toke never hurt anybody, less dangerous than vodka, but one day you get caught, a lot of people here look bad, are let down.

FRANK FARBER: You put John in the middle again. You did this to your wife, here, when you brought a broad home and fucked her right in the house, and now you're doing it to John. I got no fucking respect for you.

JOHN MAHER: You're right back to where you were when you came in here, like some fat Warner Brothers producer who thinks, "So what if I cheat on my wife? What she don't know won't hurt her. So what if I stick my dickie into three or four Vegas whores at the same time?" And like you, he's got a valid argument: "Nobody's business what you do with your body." He never snaps to the fact that it makes him a liar and a cheat! I don't think Tom Grapshi, here, would *die* if he took one beer with lunch, but I *do* think fifty other kids here, who couldn't handle it, *would* go out and drink beer and wind up on the needle—and the betrayal of all those people would *kill* Tom Grapshi!

STAN PARKINSON: I just wanted to see if I could handle it.

JOHN MAHER: Now, hear this, folks: Hippeze is a language you use when you got something you want to do. It was *more* than a little toke with you, Stan; it was a life-style you'd become used to and were too *old* for. The past year you been with us, *sure* you had troubles, but know something? You *look* healthier. Your long hair is kinda *nice* long hair now.

STAN PARKINSON: I know that—I'm testing myself.

JOHN MAHER (lapsing into his pompous white-collar drunk routine): "Whiskey is legal, everybody drinks whiskey. Winston Churchill, he drank a whole quart of brandy everyday of his life—didn't hurt *him*." (Screaming.) No, it didn't hurt Churchill, you prick, but *you* fucked up with it! (Mincing.) "I just keep the bottle there so I can look at it and prove I can handle it." What unbelievable horseshit! Stan, you took on certain responsibilities, and you take a *stand* on them! *You* know a little pot won't hurt me, but the very act jeopardizes some better values, like sending Wanda here to school, or getting Slug Mozzarella out of jail. You still think like a teen-age boy.

STAN PARKINSON: I guess I didn't want to give anything up.

JOHN MAHER (with quiet persuasion): Don't you understand? You *always* give something up! When you chippy on your wife, here, you destroy the opportunity for a good marriage. When you vote Republican you keep Nixon in office. All your semislick, hip friends will reinforce your position; they'll say, "What's wrong with a little pot?" Nothing for most people, but there's something very wrong if Cesar Chavez or Bella Abzug smokes it, they got too much at stake other than their little toke of weed. The last time you smoked pot, it went hand-in-hand with chasing groupies, and your life went *down*. You stopped, got some self-respect, you look better. Make a choice—be a hippie, get busted, and blow that good $37,000 a year gig you got with that hip clothing store.

STAN PARKINSON: The chances of me getting busted are one in twenty-five thousand.

JOHN MAHER: Right! I agree! And I ask you—what right

do you have to take that kind of gamble with Slug Mozzarella's life?

STAN PARKINSON: I guess I'm tired of this self-improvement bag.

FRANK FARBER: Then why did you take the responsibility for the Game Club? You knew you had to give up *something*.

JOHN MAHER: Somehow, I can't picture Jack Kennedy blowing a little pot, saying, "I just wanted to test myself." But I *can* picture a thousand second-rate, castrated stockbrokers, schoolteachers, and middle-class creeps saying that. Pot ain't shit, it won't hurt you—it's the *symbol*. Something wrong when a grown man like you shows all the signs of regression. You sound like a man doing time, waiting for your year's commitment to be up, so you can start in again, like the ad exec who can't pass up that one martini with the boys that'll get him started all over again, diddling on his wife.

STAN PARKINSON (in tears): I'm a trick! When I'm with hippies, I do what *they* do—when I'm here, I do what *you* do! I don't know *who* I am!

JOHN MAHER: You *do* know who you are! Why not pick your crowd, and do it all the way? We got big things to do here! Some laws to change, kids to save! We got no time for this Mickey Mouse self-indulgence. You want to get that chain of stores together you been talking about over a year, now that's *big* self-indulgence! What would be wrong with me fucking all the dumb broads that come in here? I can rationalize it, "Why not *me* do it, a guy who's not going to hurt them too much; why not take advantage of the new sexual freedom like Hugh Hefner says?" Bullshit! Because of who I *am*! Because it hurts a lot of people. You're a *father*, Stan. That means you subscribe to twenty-one years, if you're cheap, and a lifetime if you're not, of payments—emotional, intellectual, and financial payments.

RUTH PARKINSON: You know, Stan, you spent more time

the past two months worrying about how you're going to handle your end-of-the-year commitment to Delancey than you did getting your chain of stores together."

JOHN MAHER: I know I've got a good mouth. I could make a lot of money selling Chevvies, but I want to do things that make me *feel* good, important, have a place in history. Means I have to give up weed, can't fuck all the dumb cunts that stumble in here . . .

HAROLD COOK: Watch your diet (a shot at Maher's bulging waistline).

JOHN MAHER: Watch my diet, not get too fat.

JOANIE LEVIN: Cut out all the coffee . . .

MYRON BAKER: With three teaspoons of sugar—and the three packs a day . . .

FRANK FARBER: Stop getting over your head financially, buying up all this property . . .

JOHN MAHER: Watch that I don't get too many material possessions, or guys like Harold Cook will scream, "I'm making you a rich man!" If I shoot dope, I doubt there's six residents who won't fix within two weeks. You better hang out with the big buys like us, Stan. We want to take over this town in ten years! And when that Nixon depression really hits, you know what's going to happen to all the groovy jobs like yours? You wait 'til old Nixon takes the freeze off prices next April [1973] and then cattlemen push them through the ceiling, and you'll watch this economy *rock!* And you know what people are gonna cut out first? *You!* They won't be buying those pimpified $1,000 sealskin coats with mink collars. The hip culture is collapsing. Maybe you can't relate your life to the world around it. *Our* people are *not* going to be out of work. You have witnessed a miracle here! People crawl through our door, bleeding from every orifice, and today they got their health and self-respect. Are you willing to jeopardize all this? When you came here, you screamed your life was empty. You *tried* that route already, Stan, the hip, groovy, pot-smoking, groupie-chasing scene. Why don't you try another route? When are you going to push your career? Hey—it's past midnight, let's get something to eat.

CHAPTER THIRTEEN

Ron Coombs

"You can't talk-the-talk without walking-the-walk."

Ron Coombs, a twenty-seven-year-old veteran of Vietnam, has lived in Delancey Street for two years and is making plans to graduate. The movie cliché image of the dope fiend and jailbird hardly fits this all-American boy with the straw-blonde, Sundance Kid moustache. At six-foot-three and two hundred forty pounds, he moves with the easy grace of the college football star he was on his way to becoming when he got involved with crime and drugs. His account of how Delancey Street turned him around is enhanced by crisp, undramatic speech, an engaging boyish grin, and brutal candor.

RON COOMBS: I was born on a ranch outside Chico, California, and my parents separated when I was three. My mother moved to San Diego, and I stayed with Dad, leading a good clean life, hunting and fishing. When I started high school, I went south and moved in with my mother, who remarried, and I had no communication with my stepfather.

The transition to big-city life was hard. I had daytime jobs, but in the evening there was nothing to do but drink and hang out with the guys. I felt awkward in the city, so I became a follower, going to parties, vandalism. In 1960 I got into smoking weed, the thing to do. Kept on drinking,

doing what the guys did. Four years later we got into heroin
as an experiment. I thought they were lying about heroin,
like they had obviously lied about weed.

I graduated high school in 1964, working part time, so
even though I was using, I hadn't felt the need yet to go out
and steal, but got arrested for Mickey Mouse stuff, drunk,
disorderly. I moved out after too many fights with my step-
dad, so I had no one to turn to with a problem. My father
died the year I graduated, so I stayed with my sister a while,
and then got an apartment of my own. Got into dealing
heroin, made a lot of money at it, until my habit got so
heavy I was shooting up the profits. Had this chance to get
a football scholarship in Colorado and thought it would be
a good escape from drugs, because I was run-down and
started to feel rotten about myself. Sold my belongings to
buy a motorcycle for the trip, went to say goodby to my
folks, and they handed me my mail—my draft notice. So in
1967 I went in the service.

In my mind, I was finally away from drugs. After basic
training, I went to helicopter school, and then to Vietnam.
At that time, a whole lot of people weren't yet against the
war. It was still thought patriotic, you looked forward to it,
like you were really doing something. When we got over to
Vietnam, we found out it was a lot of bullshit—we were
making a lot of rich American businessmen richer, and it
gave you a real tripped-out feeling.

In Vietnam, you see a lot of things happen to your
friends and to yourself, and you've got to do a lot of things
you don't feel right about, so it was easy to get into drugs
to block those feelings out. Pure drugs were readily available.
In the U.S. heroin was maybe only 20 percent, but in 'Nam
maybe 60 percent pure.

I got shot down twice, and was the only one in the
'copter that wasn't hurt, and I got scared. By now I was
smoking opium, even more potent than heroin, and was

down from 260 to 175 pounds. They sent me to Bankok, and I didn't realize I had an opium habit, so I took no shit with me. After eight hours I started getting real sick, had convulsions. The girl I was staying with knew what was happening, and she got me two vials of heroin. I started shooting up, 50 percent pure stuff that cost me $4, $5 a day; in the States it would cost $200. I mailed a bunch of drugs home, and when I came back home in 1969, it took me five months to taper myself down to where I could function. My brother-in-law met me at the airport in Tacoma and didn't even recognize me, I looked so bad.

I was trying to get my mind together. Saw a lot of anti-Vietnam feeling, found I couldn't talk to my friends back home about the war. They were all in college, demonstrating against the war, calling me an asshole for not deserting. Made you feel completely isolated, on the outside again. Jobs were hard to come by, they ask you, "Where you been the last three years?"

Got my habit down to $75 a day and started working two jobs. When I got laid off, everything I saved went right back in my arm. Going with a girl, a square, we had a baby, were planning to get a house, a car. Then she found out what was going on, why I had no money, no drive, so I left, rather than fuck up her life as well as my own. Moved to San Francisco, stayed clean a year, working a job or two, hard physical labor, making good money, but got laid off again, had no money to send home for the baby, picked up a bad attitude and got back on the stuff again.

George, a friend, came up from San Diego, had the same background I had in Vietnam, no job, a $200 a day habit— so we went robbing. Did this for two years. After that much time, you begin to regard this as just another job. Work all day, come home at night, and cop [score for drugs].

We got busted in 1971, facing five-to-life on twenty-eight counts of armed robbery. Told the judge we got strung out in Vietnam and he wanted to send us to the V.A. [Veterans Administration] program. I looked into it and knew it was a shuck, only a matter of time before I'd be right back on the stuff. They want to get you on methadone, worse than heroin, dissolves the marrow of your bones, gives you a stomach habit like opium, and a bitch to kick, really hell.

The judge told us there were two alternative programs, Synanon and Delancey Street. My lawyer said Synanon was too rigid, and I wanted something I could slide through and get off probation. While George and I were in jail, we wrote Delancey and they sent two people to interview us. When we went up for sentencing, the judge said we could either go to jail on a five-to-life, or to Delancey Street for two years. So George and I picked Delancey just to get out of jail.

When they let us out of jail, we didn't go right to Delancey Street like we'd agreed, but stopped off at my sister's place in Oakland for one last party, drinking, smoking weed. Then George's girlfriend drove us across the bridge to Delancey Street—and it was a shock. The neighborhood blew me right out of my head. I was expecting some ghetto like the Fillmore, or one of those beat-up methadone centers or halfway houses in the shit part of town, and here I was surrounded by mansions with flower gardens. So I said to George, "Let's check this out—if we don't like it, we can go back to the car, drive to Oregon, jump probation, change our names, hide out, the whole bit." We walked up these fancy marble stairs though this huge iron gate, and there was a live band, lot of people dancing, good-looking women, and I said, "Jesus God, George, this looks all right!"

They asked us where we'd been, why we were late, and told us to sit on this bench in the front hall. The girl that drove us over, they asked her upstairs. Few minutes later she walked back down, out the door, and drove off. She told them we'd had a drink before we came over, and they told us this was against the rules, besides being late. So they had us sit on this hard bench to wear off the alcohol. After eight full hours of this, I was looking at the front door thinking, "Bullshit, I don't need these people, I'm leaving," and just at this moment they came in, took us downstairs, and told us they had to cut our hair. I asked them for just a little trim, but they shaved my whole head, which they explained they do to all the men when they first come in.

After that, I was not in too big a hurry to step out on the street—bald head, my image is gone. Couldn't go back home looking like that. Then they sat us back on the bench until the next morning, about twenty hours, telling us, "You made us wait for you, came in here smelling of liquor, now you can wait for us a while."

First they explained the rules: no drugs or alcohol, no violence, no messing with any girl in the house for at least ninety days, and after that, none of the girls under eighteen. They asked for an eighteen-month verbal committment to stay, but hell, I already had that from the judge.

They started us out "in the dishpan," emptying ashtrays, scrubbing sinks, which was kind of humiliating because I was thinking, "I got a trade, skilled roofer and carpenter—what have they got me doing this shit for?" Especially in front of a bunch of young ladies, attractive, watching me do all this with my bald head, wiping their tables after dinner.

After fifteen days of this, I was transferred to the moving company, and in those days they only had one little Ford van with three guys working it, making $300, $400 a month from jobs we picked up by word-of-mouth from squares who played Games. I decided this could be a pretty good business. A few more guys joined the crew, got more jobs, bought a lot more trucks and vans, and built the moving company to a $75,000 annual business in less than a year.

All the money paid to us for moving was kicked right back into the house. I didn't pocket the money. I was facing

five-to-life, and knew I couldn't get very far on the street
with the $50, $100 I got for a day's moving. Besides, these
people had been kind of nice to me, and I'd given them my
word, which was the only thing I really had, and could see
that the money coming in from my moving company was
going for food for the one hundred people we had living in
Arabia at that time. This stirred up a little unity, made me
feel the work I was doing was *needed* to run the house. They
told us there was no large foundation or government money.

Because I did good with the moving company, they re-
warded me with a little status, some comfort, moving me
out of the crowded dorm into my own apartment, nicely
furnished, king-size bed, inner springs, good working cable
TV, FM-AM radio, and a lot more privacy, although on
principle, there're no outside locks on any of the doors; you
can lock your room from the inside when you want privacy,
but once you leave your apartment, you don't go locking up,
like on the outside where you don't trust anybody. Like
everyone else, after I'd been there eighteen months I drew
$20 a month wam—walking-around money—so I could go to
a movie and buy a milkshake. But most of the things I
needed, like cigarettes and toilet articles, we were getting
free.

Then I got into a beef—what they call a jackpot. After
I'd been here ninety days I came up with this rationalization
that I was working hard, and unlike some of these other
lames in the house, I could handle a beer. So George and I
started phoning our girlfriends in Oakland to pick us up in
the evening, and we'd go out drinking. This went on for a
couple months. The moving business kept getting better,
maybe that's one of the reasons we didn't pocket any
moving money, because George and I were hitting these
girls up for a couple bucks.

They caught us one night and took us upstairs, half-tanked, and asked us where we'd been: "Oh, out drinking, seeing a couple girls, smoking a little weed." Now there'd been some *other* things we'd done before that, but neither of us mentioned it, and that was, George and I went out and shot some dope during the first thirty days we were in the house. And my rationalization for that was, I got eighteen months, and when that's up, I'm gone. I'll work hard for them, because it's a nice place and they're good to me—but I had no emotional commitment to the house or these people.

So we never told them about shooting dope but copped [confessed] to sneaking out, smoking weed, and the other stuff. They were obviously *concerned* about us, and told us that what they were about to do was for our own good. They put us back "in the dishpan" for sixty days, and George split—couldn't handle it. They shaved my head again, busted me off the moving crew, back into "maintenance," starting all over again, moved me out of my nice apartment on Pierce Street and had me sleeping on the floor on a mattress, because Delancey was growing, and before John bought the Russian house a few blocks away, there wasn't enough sleeping room in Arabia. They told me it would be at least six months before I could go with any girl over eighteen in the house, and gave me the really dirty jobs, cleaning sewer lines. The idea was, to impress upon me that I had given up something, and how stupid my mistake was. This was pointed out to me in Games, that if my parole officer had caught me with a beer or a joint, that's enough to violate parole and send me up from five-to-life.

In Games they started to throw in an emotional tie with the other people in the house: "Ron—don't you think we'd *all* like to go out and have a beer, smoke a joint, but a lot of people around here can't handle it, it would kill them. They see you doing it, you, the number two man on the moving crew, a role model for the younger guys, and a week later they're back with a needle in their arm. You can't tell someone to do something you don't do yourself."

At first, I didn't think Games put me through any changes, but I could see they did after about ninety days. I started taking out a lot of my frustrations in Games. The way they changed me, I was telling other guys not to smoke weed, or break other rules, and I started to realize, "What are you talking about? You're doing all these things yourself. How can you expect this guy to look up to you?" And so I began to get a terrible case of the guilts, because there were ten men in the crew role modeling to me, the way I role modeled to Mon Sandhu when I first came here.

In those early days, when there were only a hundred of us in the house, we didn't have a lot of money to spend on fun, so we had to make our own, like picnics and outings—but the main thing was the Games. We played three times a week, and one of those Games was a minion with the same group of twenty people, so after a year, you get to know these people pretty intimately.

After my first jackpot when they shaved my head and started me all over again, I had to work my way up in the moving company, build the trust of the house. And then after I'd been here a year, something weird happened. I was walking into a Game and saw Jose Batista come back after he'd split, sitting on the bench, Jose was one of the guys I'd shot dope in the house with, which is the thing I had never copped to, and I'd been carrying this guilt with me over a year, dealing with a lot of kids eighteen and under at the time. Jose gave me the high sign, "Don't worry about it, I won't cop," but by this time, I realized that this house was *mine*, and knew the consequences if the police or the newspapers, some of which were down on Delancey, found anyone shooting dope on the premises, and what this would mean to a lot of lives. So I went into my Game and was lecturing some young kid about the reason he had no friends is that no one in the house felt they could trust him, and it just flipped my gut, couldn't handle it, and told myself, "Ron, you can't talk-the-talk without walking-the-walk," and I walked out of the Game, past Jose on the bench, went upstairs, and told Mon Sandhu and the others that over a year ago Jose and I had shot some dope together in the house.

I asked myself, "Jesus—why bring this up *now?* When I'd been clean over a year?" I never snitched on anybody in my whole life, expecially myself, and I knew that by copping to this, I would be giving up a lot. But by now there were three hundred people living here, and I knew that if I ever saw a guy walking out of the house with a couple of kids to get them loaded, I would have stopped him. I guess that's the way a guy changes around here.

So they shaved my head again, for the third time, took everything away, my vehicle, status, number two man on the crew, my apartment—another sixty days of sleeping in the attic on the floor. I even lost my relationship with Lucy, one of the girls in the house, because I was an asshole, made her look bad.

After thirty days of washing dishes, I was accepted back, returned to the construction crew, but at the bottom, so all the guys I had been giving orders to were now giving orders to me. It was humiliating, hard to deal with. Lots of guys can't take the blow to their image, and split, but in six months or a year, you'll see most of them walk back through the door, sit on the bench, ask to be accepted again. In Games, they encourage you to deal with your mistakes, telling me that if I could toughen this one out, handle this humiliation, I would come up stronger, better able to make right decisions, and if the decision is wrong, you learn that, too. You run from the problem, you don't learn from it.

Finally, when I earned back the respect of the house, they invited me to one of the barber's Games, which is a mark of status because they're taking care of *business* in there. I told them I wanted to go to school, and they said, "Who the hell are *you* to want to go to school—you fucked up!" and I left that Game pretty crushed.

After I worked my way back to a foreman position and started a profitable roofing company, I went back to my barber and said I wanted to get a contractor's license because it would make a lot of money for the house, and laid it out for them in proposal form, how much it would cost, how much we could gross a month. They played a few Games with me, tested me in a business way, and gave me $600 to go to school. It took me four months to get the California State Contractor's License, which is heavy, because most guys, when they walk out of the joint or a government dope-fiend program and try something like that, it's impossible, because nobody helps, everybody looks down on them as misfits and fuck-ups, until you start believing them and give up. What we do here is raise people up, make them stronger, so that when someone on the outside looks down on you as an ex-con, you say, "Fine," and go down the street someplace else looking for work, it doesn't hurt. Our business has had an unbelievable growth; we put in new roofs, windows, move expensive furniture and art goods, and the people we work for see what a good job we do, realize we're really human.

We work hard, but we play hard too. Every weekend, I take twenty, thirty of our guys hunting and fishing in Woodland where some friends of mine have a ranch, lend us guns, decoys, we really have a good time, go down the American River in rafts, just like any workingman, only difference is, we don't have the weed, the beer, or the violence.

My commitment's been over for six months, which is kind of strange, because when I came in here, I thought,

"I'm here for eighteen months and that's it, goodby." I want to graduate, because I can't see spending the rest of my life in this kind of situation. But the contractor's license I got is for the house, and before I leave I have to train a qualified person to take over the license, and that puts a lot of responsibility on me; kind of works on you, knowing you just can't walk out the door and leave thirty people under you without training and leadership. After a few years of living clean, you get these feelings, get tied in with these people.

Now I got the opportunity to have my own roofing business through the Delancey Credit Union. The house will set me up in business, find me an apartment, help me get a car. And if I have problems with the business and can't repay the Credit Union right away, I can go to John and he'll put me in touch with his square business heads who'll tell me how to deal with these problems, give me another loan. I know I have a very good future.

Of course, John Maher is behind all this. They held these seminars every morning, where someone in the house would run it down about what Delancey was doing, for about an hour, except when John did it, once or twice a week, and then it would run three hours. First time I heard John, I thought, "Jesus, they got me in here with a bunch of *commies!*" The second time he spoke I thought I was hearing Martin Luther King. And his seminars would start to build the unity. He told us where the Foundation was going; we'd ask him questions. He got rid of a lot of my prejudices about blacks, and my ignorance, the labels they put on people.

John has a way of carrying everyone in the room. He will say something in three hours to hit all three hundred people, give them something to work on. He speaks to an audience. He can talk about the prejudiced honkies, the prejudiced blacks, the guilt people carry around. He caroms everyone, hits them with something, and when he walks out, he leaves them thinking about themselves and their actions, what they really want to do with their lives, and if their lives are kind of fucked up, how they can change it.

The reason John gets so much respect is that everyone knows he is not asking you to do anything he doesn't do himself. I got so much trust in the man, that he can ask me to do anything, I wouldn't even question it, and I never felt that way about anyone. John can relate to you, put you through changes, because he's been there himself, it's not something he's read in a book.

I'm not *afraid* of John, but I know if I try to run something under him he'll say, "Ron—quit bullshittin' me. Don't bullshit a bullshitter," and that's frightening, because you got to come right out and level with him. I've seen him in Games hit people right on the button, blow them away, put the fear of God into them, tear them down, but before they leave that Game, he'll build them back up, give them confidence, something to help them deal with that problem, because he's had that same problem, and worked through it.

I sat through a couple of Dissipations and heard John indicted by some of the directors—big-time lawyers, heavy Game players, ex-Synanon faces—about his bullheadedness, not hiring outside help to run the kitchen, buying up real estate too fast, getting over our head financially. John's fantastic under attack. Most directors in Games, if three, four people yell at them, are rat-raging at them, pretty soon they're rattled. Not John, never. I've seen twenty very heavy people like Hal Fenton and Chester Stern getting crazy on him. He'll listen, but never gets rattled.

But the thing John did that really blew my mind was when he bought the Russian mansion. He'd talked about it

for months, and it sounded nice, but we had trouble believing it. But when John actually went out and laid down
the money for this huge house in the best part of town, and
moved us in, then we realized there was just no limit to what
we could do.

CHAPTER FOURTEEN

The First Hurrah

"We're going to take over San Francisco in ten years, working within the system, same way Mayor Curley took over Boston."

John Maher is obsessed with the future. "Either we grow, or we die." His plans for Delancey Street's growth are not modest, and the possible uses of establishment politics to insure this grow are never far from his mind.

JOHN MAHER: There will be no Republican or Democratic conventions in our congressional district in which Delancey Street's political clubs are not the deciding factor. This sounds pompous, but *not* when you can turn out a larger crowd than all other factions combined. We helped get the vote out for John Burton and elected him congressman from our district by canvassing door-to-door, registering the unregistered voters, handing out stickers and literature the day before the election. We computerized all the precincts, color-coding them on huge maps. We helped the aged, the farmworkers, the women, the minorities, woke them up on election day and bused them to the polls. Come delegation-picking time, all these people will show up, and the old party hacks will have to step aside. Delancey Street packed the hall and supported the three delegates from our district to the 1974 Democratic Convention in Kansas City: John Dearman, the law partner of our friend Assemblyman Willie Brown; Anne Daley, Sheriff Hongisto's secretary and an old party war horse; Mattie Jackson, the black labor leader on the Central Labor Council.

Delancey Street will also determine the swing vote in San Francisco's next race for mayor. Most major candidates, from both parties, are friends who went to bat for us, and have put in a lot of time around here. I have six hundred fanatical volunteers waiting in the wings, and the candidate for mayor who promises the best for the people will get our support. We will canvas every district and get out the vote.

All this scares the be-Jesus out of the establishment, because we're poor people working *within* the system, and this is what these animals fear most, not radicalism, or student sit-ins.

This is why the establishment gets so terrified when I talk about using the traditional methods of Tammany Hall to achieve the just society. They don't want Mexicans, blacks, and poor whites to understand that this is *exactly* how the Jews, Irish, and Italians pulled themselves out of the ghetto. To stop people in Boston and Chicago from calling him a nigger, the Irishman had to open some saloons and funeral parlors to turn out the vote. For every grandmother whose funeral was paid for by Boston's Mayor Curley, he got a hundred votes, year in and year out.

Delancey Street's going to open saloons: one near the San Francisco *Chronicle*, one by City Hall, one in the Mexican and black districts, one in the radical-chic part of town, where we already have a restaurant-bar. In the back room of every saloon we put a computer, programmed to give the voting records and campaign contributors of all officials, all welfare and veterans benefits available in the city and state governments, all taxes, so that a man can come in and say, "My house is taxed $4,000—and everybody else on my block is taxed $2,500." So we get the computer to tell him who to bribe. Or an Italian immigrant woman comes in and says, "They arrested my son Nunzio, and I don't speak English so good." We'll help her raise hell, give her the data, find her a lawyer.

Delancey street aims to get back to the old days when a man can come into a saloon and say, "My brother's been pinched and needs a lawyer; we're from 134th Street," and the ward heeler would calculate how many votes this would mean to the Democratic party, and say, "A fine young boy like that deserves a break." Come election time, his whole family votes the straight Delancey Street ticket.

To preserve Delancey's status as a tax-exempt Foundation from being threatened by such flagrant politicking, Maher and his battery of lawyers have set up an alternative corporation, somewhat along the lines of the old CIO Political Action Committee.

JOHN MAHER: Our enemies can't threaten our tax-exempt status, because Delancey Street has never spent a cent in politics, nor is it in fact any way political. *Delancey didn't get the vote out for our congressman, or bus senior citizens to the polls. This was done by the James Michael Curley Democratic Club, the Teapot Dome Republican Club, the Alice B. Toklas Democratic Alliance, the Harriet Tubman Club, and the W. E. B. DuBois Club—of which friends of mine just happen to be president. The people heading these clubs all work out of their homes and are even members of the Republican and Democratic Central Committee in California. We even have a Communist club. Why not? We do not tell people when they come here what to think—we only insist that they* do *things and work within the framework of ethics and pragmatism. The people who come to Delancey Street for help do not head up these clubs. But they* are *registered to vote and are used as voting registrars. When they graduate from Delancey Street, they join the political party of their choice, because that's part* of their cure, to be voting citizens and work for those candidates that advocate their various political positions.

The opposition can hassle us for fifteen years. If they take away our tax-exemption on political grounds, then we will become a religion. In fact, we plan to take over empty churches—and there's going to be a lot of them, just like there's a lot of empty mansions, and going cheap. We want to take over a synagogue where Jews of good conscience could go without a mink coat, or take over a Catholic Church for those who actually *believe* in the words of the Founder. We need Protestant churches we can turn over to a good minister and tell him, "We don't agree with your bible-thumping, but you seem like an ethical man who stands fast. Why don't you take this church and preach?" We *have* to go into religions, just as we have to go into unions, politics, everything. There's no point to our work unless the world changes. Otherwise, we'll just sit here forever and merely cure the next crop of dope fiends.

What could happen on a national scale is that neighborhoods like ours will organize into community-action groups to stamp out the drug peddlers and the Mafia, working within the legal and ethical framework.

This is what terrifies the establishment—because as long as you remain *only* a dope-cure program, like these halfway houses, there's no fear you'll cure any dope fiend, or solve any of the real problems that create them. You can't cure a Puerto Rican dope fiend and send him back to live in the South Bronx. If he's *really* cured, he'd be the only sane man on his block, and this would drive him crazy.

The establishment and the right-wing nuts who control education and the textbook industry in this country, don't want poor people to realize what the Jew learned at the cost of thousands of dead and overworked bodies, what the Irish learned from the Molly Maguires hanging in the coalyards and battling the Boston Protestants, and what the

Italian—who was further blocked because he was the last to come over—only began to realize through the instrument of organized crime.

Delancey Street takes these ethnic models for success and places them on a multiracial and multiclass basis to perform the same functions as Tammany Hall and the Sons of Italy. This alarms the establishment, the social workers, the government bureaucrats, and the prison officials, because it means their days are numbered.

Second governments like this are common to the American experience. The Italian-American had been so dominated by the Mafia that it became a second government in urban "Little Italy." When I was a boy, my Irish clan was much more afraid of the local political boss than of the police. In California and the Midwest of the early 1950s, the right-wing cranks formed a second government, and folks were a lot more worried about what they thought, than what the government thought. To change society, decent people have to build an alternative and protective structure in their neighborhoods.

What is needed is the development of a new and *indigenous* philosophy to alleviate the injustices of the American state. The call of revolution must develop ideologies applicable to the experience of the North American continent, and not imported by European experiences—like the twin chimeras of Marxism-Capitalism.

Marxism has always been a joke in this country, has never produced the kind of civil liberties important to Americans and destroyed the diversity of cultures throughout Russia, Eastern Europe, and Red China. It has no current application to the American experience because of the prejudice of the vast majority of the poor against it. Marxist *principles* may have an enormous application if they can be digested in harmony with the concept of individual rights. The twofold problem of the Russian and Chinese peasant was lunch, and stop beating me, cossack. The problem of the American peasant—which is everyone below the level of advertising executive—is how to defend his sphere of personal freedom and *still* have lunch, quite a different problem.

Capitalism, on the other hand, is not an American notion, but a bourgeois concept derived from the Hanseatic League in Germany in their struggle against feudal lords. The American experience showed *other* modalities than Marxism or Capitalism—the modality of cooperation. There was no Capitalism at Plymouth Rock. Across the Great Plains, no hebes, wops, hunkies, or polacks, just people in wagon trains scared of Indians, scared to go back to where they were starving, who somehow cooperated until they reached the land of plenty.

What made America great was that it had a guaranteed annual wage for the first 150 years of its existence. Any sonofabitch who got off his ass and walked a thousand miles had forty acres. And there were free schools—land grant and homesteader colleges.

With the rise of the industrial society and the closing of the frontier, these giant gains were wiped out and replaced by the corporate pension, welfare systems, and other bullshit.

Today, if a poor person needs help and goes to the Democratic party, they refer you to the Legal Aid to get your son out of jail. After hundreds of miles of subway travel, what few benefits you do receive, if any, have little to do with getting him out of jail, but a lot more to do with perpetuating your plight in a slightly more comfortable fashion. Instead of building a works project in the good old graft sense, they put us all on the dole, what Saul Alinsky called "Welfare Colonialism."

Capitalism, which was based on the notion of free enterprise, has been destroyed. When these Chamber of Commerce clowns start pontificating, "My grandfather began with a pushcart and wound up owning Macy's," that was before income tax, sales tax, personal property tax, import tax, when some immigrant didn't have to fill out thirty-seven forms and report to fifteen commissions so he could hire a clerk. Today, somebody thinks he's a Capitalist and starts McDonald's, some conglomerate buys him out or squeezes him out.

Our merchant marine—the only one left in the world in 1945—was given away, because the big corporations find it cheaper to register the ships as Panamanian and hire Maylays to run them. Our shipyards have been given away because it's cheaper to buy from East Germans and the Japanese than to hire American workmen. It's cheaper to pay Chileans 50 cents an hour to dig copper; for that price you could put four Americans on welfare and *still* show a profit. Stockholders and big corporate manipulators who make money by exploiting foreign labor in the name of rebuilding those countries, to put Americans to work, have to create constant problems, so they hire people to *contain* those problems, rather than *solve* them. It is insane that in 1945 there was only one nation—ours—whose industrial base was intact; that this nation should wake up to find huge portions of its population unemployed, its cities and schools not functioning, its agricultural base eroded in favor of large farms, its merchant fleet destroyed—the monopolists have done this.

The establishment does not want us to discuss these realities, but to get hot over, "Can I smoke marijuana?" or, "Is it okay to wear jockey shorts made from an American flag?" *There's* a real burning issue while millions starve in New York! I never see these liberals throw a picket line around a tough, gangster dominated union hiring hall that could give blacks a job tomorrow; they play it safe by picketing a college to start a Swahili department because if they picket the Mafia, they'll get their legs broke. We've got to sweep these mock-revolutionary assholes right out of our goddam way so's we can get a clear shot at the enemy! If you jump up and denounce anybody, forty-seven so-called radical groups will scream, "You said ladies instead of women!" "What about gay people?" "Don't Armenians get a break here?" You have to be the *Messiah* to change anything, which is precisely the design of the establishment— keep the suckers grappling with unissues, and in the meantime, we'll cut up all the fuckin' money.

What keeps the establishment powerful, when they're really weak, is the Marxist-Capitalist argument; everything is defined in terms the establishment can *defend*.

People began to accept both the Marxist and Capitalist myths as realities. The right-wing cranks have for so long owned the textbook industry, that educated people no longer understand that the entire history of this nation has been *classic* class warfare from it's inception. The pilgrims were a bunch of cranks who came here because nb one in England wanted to put up with their boring bullshit. We've had class warfare from the Whiskey Rebellion, the Civil War, the Draft Riots, Coxey's Army, the Molly Maguires, the I.W.W., the Republic Steel Massacre, and the Black Panthers. People think the Panthers and women's lib are *new*, but this is the chronological history of the United States—the Philadelphia Riots, the Irish and Italian wars against the natives of New York City, the Catholics versus the Wasps for control of Boston, the war between mine owners and the United Mine Workers.

But through their control of textbooks and the public schools, the right has subtly obliterated this history of class warfare, so that when the left attacks, it attacks not the existing evil, but only the conceptualized evil that the right has applied through propaganda. And when the right attacks the left, it only attacks the vision promulgated by the left. We need an American kid to shout, "The emperor ain't got no goddamn clothes on!"

There's a different argument for Americans than Marxism versus Capitalism, and that's more like the Christians versus the Romans—enlighted humanism and ethical attack as opposed to warring ideologies. This is *crucial* to change in the U.S., where the long-range social advances were produced by people like Martin Luther King, Malcolm X, and the Wobblies—not by doctrinaire ideologues of either the old or new left, and certainly not by fragmented student-radical-hippie groups of the sixties, which were foolishly thought to be serious vehicles for social change.

Hippies began when blacks and Latins forced their way into schools and jobs. A small Bohemian enclave that had always existed in America suddenly sprang out into instant culture. Now any sane person looking at this dispassionately would say, "I see—there's not enough schools and jobs, or roles for people, so as you place blacks in schools and jobs, the system must squeeze out the whites." But to keep the whites from screaming. "Where's our jobs?" you convince these tripped-out little bastards they are dropping out in *protest*, like some romantic Baudelaires. Then nobody will notice there's no jobs for them, and we can create hundreds more jobs for bleeding hearts and dimwit social workers running around assisting them, and getting paid for it, in an effort to keep the middle-classes employed, so they will not pool their brains with working-class brawn.

As the winos—the residuals of Prohibition and the Depression—all died out in New York, and there were no more hobos, this same neighborhood was filled with hippies. Everyone thought this was a new phenomenon, but there were *always* hobos in the Bowery, only instead of head shops with groovy roach-holders and love beads, it was the *Hobo News* and Sammy's Bowery Follies. Just a different sales pitch. These poor cripples laying around Eighth Street didn't understand, that in a society that had sold out its productive base to gain profits for a few, it was necessary to disguise the fact that the hippies are the hobos of the sixties.

Ten years ago, they thought the students were harbingers of social revolution. Today, the media runs endless articles, "What Happened to the Student Movement?" What movement? It was a great *party!* The revolutionary intentions of groups that shit on the dean's desk are highly suspect. What was Selma? Not students, but a bunch of tough old blacks who had stood with King for ten years. The importation of a lot of Jewish kids for an exciting summer vacation don't mean shit, they're all going home next Monday. For students, the fun went out of the fad, and people with some limited understanding of how to reform education and end the war, lost interest as soon as they weren't going to be drafted, like a lot of working people in the twenties and thirties lost their fervor for social justice when they got guaranteed annual wages. The student movement was kept alive by middle-class liberals, thank God, who kept them in the news and made them *causes célèbres*. But as soon as liberals got tired of students and went on to another tactic, the whole movement collapsed. Students were good pawns for sensible radicals and libertarian conservatives who wanted to end the war. Some of these student leaders later freaked out over that fifteen-year-old Maharaj Ji. I suspect that if Uncle Hitler came to the Houston Astrodome with a great rock band, flashing light shows, groovy uniforms, back to the land and strength through joy, some of those poor lame cocksuckers would have put on a swastika.

The only thing the student movement produced that affected working people is more classes in Swahili, macramé, pebble collecting, and tarot. Let's get back to engineering schools to recycle the economy so that our waters aren't covered with oil. All these sensory-awareness, astrology, I

Ching, naval-gazing fads, they're cute hobbies. Old-time religions aren't working anymore and you don't get a large
Baptist turnout where you rant and rave and get a cheap
peak experience. So from this opiate of the masses comes a
new opiate, "groovy-freeness," which is only a way for the
middle-class to get laid without guilt, what the proletariate
and the aristocracy have managed throughout history. "I
never really felt like a person until someone touched me in
a mudbath." Well, God bless'em! Step aside, we've got a
revolution to make.

Anyone in New York who doubts we're ready for a revolution should take a walk from 96th Street and 3rd Avenue,
up to 125th Street, bear right and cross the Willis Avenue
Bridge up to 3rd Avenue, straight up to the Bronx. You will
have passed a million people—blacks, Puerto Ricans, Irish,
and Italians, not a hippie among them, all working class. If
you have *completed* that walk, if you've been armed, swift,
and have survived, ask yourself, "Do these people give a fuck
about the American state?" No. "Are they ready for a revolution?" Yes. But nice liberals want to visit *New York* magazine and go to Greenwich Village and play house. And they
say, "What's happening, Andy Warhol?" Now he's cute,
but what *I* want to know is, what's happening, Mr. Twin
Towers, down on the waterfront? Is the Cuban gang going
to be strong enough to attack the Italians in ten years?
That's where the change is!

These same nice liberals actually believed that basic re-
forms would come out of Watergate to ward off this revolution, just as Roosevelt's New Deal turned aside the impend-
ing revolution after the Depression. Watergate was nothing
but internecine warfare between the Republican and Democratic parties to see who will emerge in control. Nothing
new. When I was a kid, and poor, senile old Eisenhower
came in, the cry was, "Twenty years of treason is over! The
pinkos who sold out China to the Reds and killed us in

Korea, the Alger Hisses who betrayed us at Yalta are gone, and a New Era has begun!" When I was in jail and Kennedy was elected, it was a New Frontier, then with Johnson the Great Society. Now they're tricking us again! Lynch Nixon in the name of reform, and announce, "We're ready for a New Era in American politics."

The social revolution crucial to America will not come about through the Republican or Democratic hacks in Washington any more than it will through thirties' radicals and sixties' students. People must understand that power bases like Delancey Street and an economy that provides these small enclaves with its own self-fueling system, without help from the government and large foundations, are the only way that enough strength can be developed to make change.

We are teaching legislators, criminal justice committees, and reform groups how to start Delancey Streets that take on the unique personalities of their leaders and their communities. They come from New York, Alaska, San Diego, Detroit, and Arkansas. We tell them, "Stay a couple of weeks—we'll put you up, as long as you don't use alcohol, drugs, or violence. Talk to anyone you like, eat with us, see how we do it. If you have a moral issue, we will support you." The head of the French drug program, Claude Orsel, is sending French prisoners to Delancey Street in September 1975, so that other countries can see how we've built, not just an alternative to the prison system, but a working model to improve the tenor of *all* society.

Besides these good people who want to use us as a guideline, we also get those who want to co-opt us for their own limited ends, and copy us out of existence. National bigname politicians come here, shake a couple of black hands, and all say the same thing, "John, can we do this in our city without *you* there? Or your friends? On our own?" And you can see right away that they don't want a Delancey Street in their city. They want a manipulable piece of machinery. So we tell this senator from New York, "Why not start a Delancey in Manhattan *with* us there?"

"And they say, "No, it's got to be the people in the district."

"You mean the people that vote for *you*, but that's not Delancey, because we'll step on your face if you don't take the moral position."

Then they say, "Well—you people are great and we love you, but you don't meet the special needs of our community," when what they *mean* is, "I can't count on you not to fight me in my district."

They want to copy the form without the essence. If a vintner with a bad vineyard were to copy Lafitte Rothschild, a non-wine-drinking public like Ireland wouldn't know the difference: "It's the same thing, much less expensive, and you can get a lot more of it." They copied Synanon until they destroyed it, confusing the public as to what a halfway house was. They did the same thing to mental health. A hundred years ago, Dorothea Dix (social and penal reformer, 1802–1887) was big throughout the nation. What they did in response to her agitation for reform of mental institutions was to take down the signs reading "Insane Asylum" and replace them with signs reading "State Hospital." Then they changed the guards' uniforms from grey to white and called them attendants instead of guards. They did the same in prisons, changing the name from penitentiary to reformatory. Everything remained exactly the same, except this proliferation of bureaucracy, like in those old Peter Sellers movies where he has a picture on the wall of Stalin, backed by a picture of Hitler, and depending on whose armies advance, he just flips the picture.

That's what the government will do with Delancey Street when they see we're a success—fund three cranks in Cleveland and tell them, "Start a program exactly like it." This is the mistake of American foreign policy, and before us, British foreign policy. Five crazed Englishmen would wander into an African tribe and decide to give them a parliament. Then these Bantus, used to doing their own number, who could have perhaps developed a democracy applicable to their own culture, are all sitting around in parliamentary wigs, speaking Oxford English to some tribesman on trial for stealing a sheep in reprisal for a murder committed in 1720—and no one saw anything strange or wrong about this for twenty years! The U.S. goes into Latin America, starts banana plantations, tin mines, and decides these peasants need a Congress, tape recorders, Nixon, and try to *duplicate*. These people always miss the point—that different forms can be just as effective. What is necessary is organic growth. They further cannot comprehend that there is no *end* to growth. The bureaucratic mind seizes on every opportunity for success as being ultimate: "If we only use group therapy, or methadone, *that* will solve the problem," not realizing that therapies we apply to the 1970s may not apply to the 1990s.

Delancey expects as an institution, like the Christians, Communists, or Muslims, there will be a great pull within the movement to view everything in the light of its own success as being good—and at that point, the movement becomes corrupt. One of the psychic tricks that intellectuals have used to prevent real change is the argument, "Sixty years from now, you'll be just as corrupt as the labor unions." But the unions represented a great advance in the thirties. Now, many are corrupt, and will have to go, or change. That doesn't mean the unions weren't needed. Delancey is not the ultimate solution to the problems of crime, addiction, or the organization of the poor. We will have to go some day, just as the monarchy had to go, and the insane way we manage our cities will have to go. Meanwhile, we're just one more advance in the evolutionary change toward a sane society.

We offer a reality-example of how to build a crucial alliance among those groups that have always supported Delancey and have been most receptive to its ideas—Roman Catholic hard-hat labor leaders, black community organizers, and smart, rich Jews. The mention of such an alliance would have been unthinkable ten years ago, when people were still dealing in pipe dreams and liberals sat around mouthing glorified generalities about the military-industrial complex. Now the country is ripe for such an alliance because we have found that we are all in this sinking American boat together.

The interests of all these groups are identical. The Jew has never been safe in a gentile country, even in America where the Jew will be destroyed in different ways than in Europe—through assimilation and the destruction of their traditional values. At the same time, the minimal anti-Jewish prejudice will not disappear. In thirty years the Jew will no longer have the support of the Jewish community for his businesses and to scratch his back *via* the "old-boy" system. Their names will all be changed to Ian Carstairs and Bruce Peterson, and they will not patronize Hymie's Bail Bonds because, like Kissinger, they will no longer think of themselves as Jews. But the prejudice that keeps them out of the upper echelons of corporate finance and the best country clubs will not disappear.

Delancey got most of its private donations from perceptive, Bernard-Baruch-type Jews—as opposed to the Beverly Hills clown—who sees in us an astounding parallel, and a chance to invigorate themselves. No Jew who came up the hard way in America looks at us and fails to see that the struggle of Delancey Street, parallels, on a multiracial basis, the struggle of the Jews. Also, the ethical premise on which Judaism is founded, the Ten Commandments, is no different from the ethical basis of Delancey Street. The perceptive Jew thinks, "Maybe I better make friends with these nuts, because you can never tell when America is going to start in on the Jew." And they're starting in, when a Pentagon general talks about the influence of Jewish banks on foreign policy, and Congress betrays the State of Israel. The Jew had best be friends with the gentile poor who share his condition. Then he will always be safe. Some wealthy Jews remember what it meant to be a Jew under Hitler, and can sympathize with the blacks and poor whites.

This nation is now ripe for an alliance between ethnic hard-hats and ghetto blacks. When we threw a picket line around the biggest hotel in San Francisco to support the Irish Republic and had blacks and Chicanos carrying signs, "English, let the I.R.A. go!" we saw Irish cops, twenty years on the force, come over and embrace these black pickets. If this was a peace march, the pickets might have got their heads bashed, but you could see in the Irish sergeant's face, "These niggers are standing up for *our* rights!" And when the unions saw our blacks on the picket line supporting the Sears strikers, they felt obligated to give us a few jobs.

The question of Ulster affects twenty million hard-hats in the U.S. for primitive and emotional reasons because their grandfathers were driven to this country by the British Army. This is one of the issues through which the American hard-hat will finally be made to see that their destiny is the same as the blacks'. When every Irishman in Pittsburgh sits up and says, "They are treating that nigger down the block the same way they are treating my cousin Seamus in Belfast," this means an awakening in the United States.

This alliance has consistently been opposed by academics, government bureaucrats, and hair-splitting radicals from the thirties who have failed so long and so miserably in bringing about any real social change in America. To these bumbling ineffectuals, what you *say* is far more important than what you *do*. If your cured fifty lepers, but spoke like a hard-hat, Southerner, or black—the three maligned elements in the culture—they would pay you no mind. But if you can express humanistic drivel in a language acceptable to that vast band that confuses impotence with morality, they call it open-mindedness, and cheer, whether you accomplish anything or not.

These are the same people who oppose Delancey Street and run their mouth about our "high failure rate, and this pompous authoritarian who runs the joint and likes to get his name in the papers—and there's a hierarchy, everybody doesn't even vote." Lames from the Welfare Board tell me, "John, you're too aggressive." "You're too harsh on the addict," says the functionary who worked at Attica Prison. "What about all the groovy kids who don't want to do all these things you tell them—like *work*—but just want to sit around making candles?" says some yo-yo trained in the Berkeley School of Social Work, who would no doubt walk up to Joe Hill and Eugene Debs and ask, "Just how many of you Wobblies are mature, liberated individuals without sexual hang-ups?"

Northern liberals co-opted the civil rights and antiwar movements without articulating a position in terms that Archie Bunker could understand. The most horrifying thing about the hard-hats who were beating up long-haired protesters in New York, was that it was Archie Bunker's kid, not Jerry Rubin or Bobbie Dylan, who was going to die in Vietnam. Look at the casualty list, and you know who's dead? Blacks, Roman Catholic poor, and Southern Baptist boys, *that's* who's fucking dead! And *that* should have been the rhetoric of the antiwar movement because that's something ironworkers and dock-wallopers can comprehend. But that wasn't fashionable in cocktail party circles, where liberal-intellectuals whined that Archie Bunker and the shit-kickers who elected Wallace and Nixon were against them. So the liberals heightened the hatred between blacks and whites, while claiming to try and solve the conflict, when they couldn't be honest and admit they only took on causes that immediately gratified their own view of themselves.

The one who *should* have headed those peace marches, and *would* have, if handled right, was the construction worker who lost two kids in Vietnam, pays all the taxes, does all the work; they scare him that the blacks want his job, and when bank rates go up, they freeze him out, lay him off. *He's* the guy on the line. If the liberals had put out their hand to him in the Democratic Convention of 1968, the working class might have stood with them. But now they might turn to Wallace and Reagan because they've nowhere else to go. They are isolated, losing their jobs, their mortgages are due, they live in a vast welfare state created by big corporations that exploit foreign labor which is used to threaten their jobs. They've been held in narrow provincialism by the kind of media they're exposed to, their religions are dying, their families are breaking up. Archie Bunker is in a state of shock because his hero Nixon stands unfrocked, prices have skyrocketed, and he knows we have lost the first war in our history. How will he react to this? Whoever comes to Archie in his time of need and says, "We stand with you," will get his vote. He has proven himself time and again on the battlefields, in the labor struggles, and despite his ignorance, is attuned to certain qualities like independence and loyalty, unlike the liberals who can be counted on to knuckle under and sell you out.

If liberal-intellectuals extend to Archie Bunker the hand of friendship and support, the hard-hat can become *radicalized*. But if they continue to revile him with their cocktail party chatter and annoy him with neo-Marxist jargon, then the hard-hat will turn to Wallace and Reagan who will start the Joe McCarthy bullshit all over again of "twenty years of treason" and how we lost the war in Vietnam because we were sold out by intellectuals, pinkos, hippie perverts, longhairs, Jewish pornographers, and the Eastern-elite-left-wing-Harvard-Commie-fruit press.

The end of the Vietnam War is symbolic that the time has come to cement this alliance. The economic crisis, the rise of crime, all contribute to this being the precise historical moment for this fundamental change. When the economy collapses, the middle class that don't think they're peasants because they go to Vegas once a year and own a color TV, can no longer be distracted by the toys they can't afford. They can't save up for the motor launch—now they got to worry about the *sandwich*, and getting mugged. For protection, they turn to the traditional bastions of law 'n' order and find they not only don't work, but are illegal and corrupt themselves. I don't mean Wallace or Nixon because they already *expect* them to be whores, but the local cop, the local hospital that's deteriorating, with forty people lined up for emergency treatment.

Once we cement this alliance, we can walk over these bums in the establishment because they are yellow and weak without their fighting force, which has always been the hardhats and minorities, the one's who got it in Vietnam. We will ally ourselves with those among the rich and powerful who understand that if current racial and penal injustices are not corrected, they will be impoverished by the taxation required to maintain the bureaucracy. They will realize that the only way to prevent violent revolution and English-style poverty in America is to support community groups like ours, and stand fast.

The unenlightened among the rich and powerful will laugh at us, the way they laughed at the Chinese agrarians, at Martin Luther King's people refusing to ride the bus in Montgomery. These complacent fools will laugh, just as they did at the Jews when they tried to run an organic cabbage farm and messed it up the first few years because they were shopkeepers. And then one day they will wake up, just as the white Protestant woke up in New York about 1870 and said, "All these dumb Irish bastards, they got this thing they call Tammany Hall—and they *run* this city!" And some of these dumb Irishmen say to E. L. Harriman, "Guess what—you want to keep on being a railroad big shot? You're gonna march in the St. Patrick's Day parade and take down all them signs that say, 'No Irish Need Apply,' and go tell your friend Mr. Vanderbilt to build some libraries in our neighborhood, or there's going to be a strike at the Vanderbilt sweat shop and the Amalgamated Motherfuckers of America."

These rich fools will wake up and understand that the senior citizens can be bused to the polls by the convicts, that former addicts can do volunteer work for the women's movement, and that blacks, once isolated in ghettos, now have allies and friends among the hard-hats. And on that day we'll tell them to stop the nonsense or we'll be rid of them. They will sneer and say, "Tell me jokes—the church is behind us."

We'll tell them, "The church only got four votes."

They will say, "We got the unions in back of us."

We'll tell them, "Most of the unions can't turn out a vote anymore. The working people are with us because they really believe in the union movement. Take it to the polls, Buster—and we will *smash* you!"